Directory of Repositories of

FAMILY HISTORY
IN
NEW HAMPSHIRE

SCOTT E. GREEN

CLEARFIELD

Printed for
Clearfield Company, Inc. by
Genealogical Publishing Co., Inc.
Baltimore, Maryland
1993

Reprinted for
Clearfield Company, Inc. by
Genealogical Publishing Co., Inc.
Baltimore, Maryland
1994, 1997

International Standard Book Number: 0-8063-4671-X

Made in the United States of America

TABLE OF CONTENTS

iii

INTRODUCTION

The purpose of this book, DIRECTORY OF REPOSITORIES OF FAMILY HISTORY
IN NEW HAMPSHIRE, is to provide a list of institutions which have family
papers and other material which would be of interest to genealogists and
other scholars.
   The entries are organized by counties and then by municipality. Under
each county, I list the addresses and telephone numbers of the Registrar of
Deeds and the Registrar of Probate. With each town or city, I list the
first founding date of the community, the mailing address and the telephone
number of the city or town clerk and, the previous names of the community.
Then I list the various institutions within the community that have holdings.
   Those communities which are cities have an "*" in front of their names
and the clerk should be styled City Clerk.
   In some towns and cities, the holdings of local historical and genealogical groups are located within other institutions (usually public libraries). Access to those particular collections are usually controlled by
the host institution's staff. I merely list the name of the local historical or genealogical group then cross-reference to the host institution.
   In New Hampshire the normal practice is for town and city records to be
located at the local clerk's office. Records which predate the Revolution
are normally found either at the state's archives or the New Hampshire
Historical Society. However, some pre-Revolutionary records may be found
either at the county or municipal level because the state has no power to
compel local governments to comply with state law which requires pre-
Revolutionary records to be deposited at the State Archives.
   It must be understood that there is very little financial support for
the management of historic records in New Hampshire. The New Hampshire
State Archives ranks 50th in terms of funding from the state. Towns and
cities usually do not have local historical agencies, though infrequently
they may give annual donations to a local historical society, and occasion-
ally they do designate someone as the town historian or the town archivist.
These positions are usually honorary. There are many historic district com-
missions in the state. These are concerned with zoning regulations and
identifying the sites to be placed on the national register of historic
sites. Their files usually have little material relevant to the needs of
genealogists.
   On the other hand, town clerks and the local public librarians usually
have the names and telephone numbers of contact people in the local historical society and names of local genealogists who might be available for
consultation and research.
   I suspect that more historical societies than I note keep their collections at the public libraries. I was not able to reach every single public
library and every historical society in the state because they never res-
ponded to my telephone calls or correspondence.
   I do not list every historical society or public library that I con-
tacted. In the case of the historical societies there are three reasons:
   1. They do not have any holdings in family history.
   2. They have little or no records on their holdings at this time so
they do not know what they do have.
   3. The collections are really personal property of the members of the
society rather than the society's own holdings.
   As for the public libraries, they do not have a family or local history collection beyond a few scattered volumes on town or family history.
   I also do not list research fees. Most historical societies, because
they are volunteer groups, do not have a fee schedule. Individuals within
the society may and do charge. The larger historical groups such as the
New Hampshire Historical Society, the Manchester Historical Association,
and the Portsmouth Athenaeum do charge modest fees for the daily use of
their libraries and for research that takes more than a half-hour. The
researcher should ask about these fees because they may be waived or re-
duced under certain circumstances.
   Photocopying fees are always to be expected at any facility.
When I use the term "some town records" this usually refers only to

1

annual town reports, especially in the holdings of the smaller public libraries. The term "small book collection" means that there are fewer than
twenty volumes in a particular collection either on town or family history.
However, these collections frequently have locally published titles as well
as a few unpublished manuscripts not found elsewhere in public repositories. My bibliography is a list of reference works that focus on New
Hampshire data. I also list the publications of those genealogical societies whose publications are concerned with local genealogy.

The publications of local historical societies are listed with the entries of the societies that publish them. Unless a newsletter has a dis-
tinctive name, I refer to the publication as newsletter. Whenever poss-
ible I also note book titles that are currently in print.

The area code for all New Hampshire telephone numbers is 603.

BELKNAP COUNTY

Registrar of Deeds
64 Court St.
Laconia 03246
Telephone 524-3570

Registrar of Probate
P. O. Box 1343
Laconia 03247
Telephone 524-0903

ALTON (1796)
P. O. Box 637, Town Hall, Alton 03809, Telephone 875-2101.
Previous names: New Durham Gore.

Alton Historical Society, P. O. Box 536, Alton 03809, no telephone.
Hours: By appt.
Holdings: Small book collection.

Gilman Library, Main St., Box 960, Alton 03809, Telephone 875-2550.
Hours: Winter: Mon. through Wed. 2-8, Fri. 9-5, Sat. 9-12. Summer: Mon.
through Wed. 12-8, Fri. 9-5, Sat. 9-12.
Holdings: Vertical file. Index of local family names. Cemetery lists.
Vital statistics list.

BARNSTEAD (1727)
P. O. Box 11, Town Hall, Center Barnstead 03225, Telephone 269-4631.

Barnstead Historical Society, P. O. Box 11, Town Hall, Center Barnstead
03225, no telephone.
Hours: By appt.
Holdings: Cemetery lists. Files on local homes. Files on families.

BELMONT (1859)
P. O. Box 310, Belmont 03220, Telephone 267-8300.
Previous names: Gilmanton, Upper Gilmanton.

Belmont Historical Society-see Belmont Public Library.

Belmont Public Library, P. O. Box 97, Belmont 03220, Telephone 267-6525.
Hours: Winter: Mon. & Wed. 1-5, Tues. & Thur. 12:30-7:30, Sat. 9-12.
Summer: Mon. 1-5, Tues. & Thur. 12:30-7:30, Wed. 1-7:30.
Holdings: Some town records. Small book collection. Includes holdings of
Belmont Historical Society.

CENTER HARBOR (1797)
P. O. Box 140, Center Harbor 03226, Telephone 253-4561.

Center Harbor Historical Society, P. O. Box 74, Center Harbor 03226, no
telephone.
Hours: By appt.
Holdings: Small book collection. Town records.

James E. Nichols Memorial Library, Box 1339, Center Harbor 03226, Telephone 253-6950.
Hours: Winter: Mon. 2-5, Wed. 2-8, Sat. 10-4. Summer: Mon., Wed. & Fri.
3-8.
Holdings: Some town records. Vertical files.

GILFORD (1812)
Town Hall, 47 Cherry Valley Rd., Gilford 03246, Telephone 524-3286.
Previous names: Gunstock Parish.

Gilford Public Library, 2 Belknap Mt.Rd.Gilford 03246,Telephone 524-6042.

3

Hours: Mon., Wed., Fri. 9-6, Tues & Thur. 9-8, Sat. 9-12 (no Sat. hrs. in summer).
Holdings: Town records. Family files. Includes holdings of the Thompson-Ames Historical Society of Gilford.

Thompson-Ames Historical Society of Gilford-see Gilford Public Library.

GILMANTON (1727)
P. O. Box 555, Gilmanton 03237, Telephone 267-6726.
Previous names: Gilmantown.

Gilmanton Historical Society, P. O. Box 236, Gilmanton 03237, no telephone
Hours: By appt.
Holdings: Some town records. Files on the Cogswell, Page and Varney families.

*Laconia (1855)
P. O. Box 489, Laconia 03246, Telephone 527-1265.
Previous names: Meredith Bridge.

Laconia Historical Society, P. O. Box 1126, Laconia 03247, no telephone.
Hours: By appt.
Holdings: Cemetery lists. Some municipal records.

Laconia Public Library, 695 Main St., Laconia 03246, Telephone 524-4775.
Hours: Mon. through Fri. 9-8, Sat. 9-4.
Holdings: Small book collection. Microfilm of local newspaper LACONIA CITIZEN. File of several defunct newspapers. Some municipal records.

White Mountain National Forest, P. O. Box 638, Laconia 03247,Telephone 528-8721.
Hours: Mon. through Fri. 8-4:30.
Holdings: Records of household and land ownership in towns such as Livermore, Landass and Landaff being taken over by the White Mountain National Forest.

MEREDITH (1748)
41 Main St., Meredith 03253, Telephone 279-4538.
Previous names: Bear Island, New Salem, Palmer's Town, Stone Dam.

Meredith Historical Society, P. O. Box 920, Meredith 03253, no telephone.
Hours: July through August Sat. 1-4 and by appt.
Holdings: Cemetery records. Some town records. Files on the Wyatt, Carlton, Rollins and North families.

Meredith Public Library, Box 808, Main St., Meredith 03253, Telephone 279-4303.
Hours: Tues. & Wed. 10-8, Thur. 8-5, Fri. 8-7, Sat. 10-2.
Holdings: Files on local families. Small book collection. Some town records. File of local newspaper.MEREDITH NEWS.

NEW HAMPTON (1765)
P. O. Box 538, New Hampton 03256, Telephone 744-8454.
Previous names: Moultonborough Addition.

Gordon-Nash Library, P. O. Box 549, Main St., New Hampton 03256, Telephone 744-8061.
Hours: Mon. through Fri. 10:30-9, Sat. 10-12.
Holdings: File on the Drake family. Small book collection. Town records. Church records. Includes the holdings of the New Hampton Historical Society.

New Hampton Historical Society-see Gordon-Nash Library.

SANBORNTON (1770)
P. O. B.v 124, Sanbornton 03269, Telephone 286-4034.
Previous names: Crochtown, Sanborntown.

Sanbornton Historical Society, P. O. Box 2, Sanbornton 03269, no telephone.
Hours: By appt.
Holdings: Sanborn family papers. List of Revolutionary and Civil War veterans.

Sanbornton Public Library, Box 88, Sanbornton 03269, Telephone 286-8288.
Hours: Tues. & Fri. 9-4, Wed. & Thur. 1-8,
Holdings: Small book collection. Clipping file.

TILTON (1869)
145 Main St., Tilton 03276, Telephone 286-4425.
Previous names: Bridge Village, Sanbornton Bridge.

Hall Memorial Library, 18 Park St., Tilton 03276, Telephone 286-8971.
Hours: Winter: Mon. & Wed. 10-8, Tues. & Thur. 11-8, Fri. 10-6, Sat. 11-2.
Summer: Mon. & Fri. 11-4, Tues. & Wed. 11-8, Sat. 11-2.
Holdings: Some town records. Vertical files.

New Hampshire Old Graveyard Association, 7 Maple Court, Tilton 03276, no
telephone.
Hours: By appt.
Holdings: List of 4,000 cemeteries in New Hampshire.

Tilton Historical Society, Town Hall, Tilton 03276, no telephone.
Hours: By appt.
Holdings: Town records.

CARROLL COUNTY

Registrar of Deeds
County Administration Building
Ossipee 03864
Telephone 539-7751

Registrar of Probate
County Administration Building
Ossipee 03864
Telephone 539-4123

ALBANY (1766)
P. O. Box 1767, Conway 03818, Telephone 447-2877.
Previous name: Burton.

BARTLETT (1790)
RFD 1, Box 50, Intervale 03845, Telephone 356-2300.

Bartlett Public Library, Box 366, Bartlett 03812, Telephone 374-2755.
Hours: Winter: Mon. & Wed. 9-5 and 7-9, Tues & Fri. 9-5, Thur. 9-3,
Summer: Mon. & Wed. 2-5 and 7-9, Tues. & Fri. 2-5.
Holdings: Vertical file. Vital statistics from 1700's to 1850's. File of
local newspaper, AMONG THE CLOUDS.

BROOKFIELD (1769)
P. O. Box 756, Sanbornville 03872, Telephone 522-3231.
Previous names: Raby.

CHATHAM (1767)
HCR, Box 241, Center Conway 03813, no telephone.

Chatham Historical Society, Box 242, Center Conway 03813, no telephone.
Hours: By appt.

Holdings: Town records. Vital statistics list. Small book collection. Publications: CHATHAM TIMES PAST AND PRESENT (quarterly newsletter, $6 annual membership.

CONWAY (1765)
Box 70, Center Conway 03813, Telephone 447-3822.
Previous names: Pequawket, Pigwacket.

Conway Historical Society-see Conway Public Library.

Conway Public Library, Box 2100, Main St., Conway 03818-2100, Telephone 447-5552.
Hours: Mon.-Thur. 10:30-8:30, Fri. and Sat. 10:30-5:30, Sun. 1-4 (Oct.-May only).
Holdings: Large book collection. Large collection of regimental history. File of NEW HAMPSHIRE AGRICULTURE. Town records of Albany, Conway, Eaton and Madison. Nine local newspapers on file. Records of First Congregational Church of Conway. Map collection. Cemetery records. County records. Includes holdings of Conway Historical Society.

North Conway Public Library, Main St., Box 409, North Conway 03860, Telephone 356-2961.
Hours: Mon., Tues., & Thur. 2-5:30, Wed. 10-12 and 2-5:30, Fri. 2-8.
Holdings: Small book collection. Some town records. Files of local newspapers, NORTH CONWAY REPORTER and CONWAY SUN.

EATON (1700)
P. O. Box 42, Eaton Center 03832, Telephone 447-2846.

EFFINGHAM (1778)
P. O. Box 48, So. Effingham 03882, Telephone 539-7551.
Previous names: Freetown, Leavitts Town.

Effingham Free Public Library, RFD 1, Box 406, Center Ossipee 03814, no telephone.
Hours: Thur. 7-9.
Holdings: Some town records. Small book collection.

Effingham Historical Society, P. O. Box 33, South Effingham 03882, no telephone.
Hours: By appt.
Holdings: Papers of Dearborn, Potter, and Taylor families. Small diary collection. Small book collection. Records of local women's clubs.

FREEDOM (1831)
P. O. Box 51, Freedom 03836, Telephone 539-6323.
Previous Names: North Effingham.

Freedom Public Library, Box 159, Freedom 03836, Telephone 539-5176.
Hours: Tues. 6-8, Wed. 10-12, Thur. 12-3, Fri. 1-4, Sat. 2-4.
Holdings: Some town records. Vertical files.

HART'S LOCATION (1772)
Rt. 302, Hart's Location 03812, no telephone.

JACKSON (1771)
P. O. Box 336, Jackson 03846, Telephone 383-6248.
Previous names: Adams, Gilman Grant, New Madbury, Rogers Grant, Treadwell Grant, Wentworth Grant.

Jackson Historical Society, P. O. Box 8, Jackson 03846, no telephone.
Hours: By appt.
Holdings: Some town records. Clipping files.

Jackson Public Library, P. O. Box 276, Jackson 03846, Telephone 383-9731.

Hours: Winter: Tues. 11-4, Thur. 11-4 and 7-9, Summer: Tues. 10-4, Thur.
10-4 and 7-9.
Holdings: Small book collection. Several files on local families.

MADISON (1852)

P. O. Box 248, Madison 03849, Telephone 367-9931.

Madison Historical Society, P. O. Box 9, Madison 03849, Telephone 367-4867.
Hours: By appt.
Holdings: Revolutionary and Civil War veterans records. Pre-1900 death and
burial certificates. Town records. Mortgage transactions.

Madison Town & School Library, Box 240, Madison 03848, Telephone 367-8545.
Hours: Winter: Mon., Thur., & Fri. 1-4, Tues. 1-5, Wed. 12-3, Sat. 9-5.
In summer additional hours on Tues. 7-9.
Holdings: Some town records. Records of defunct Madison High School.

MOULTONBOROUGH (1763)

P. O. Box 1550, Moultonborough 03254, Telephone 476-5757.
Previous names: Long Island.

Moultonborough Historical Society-see Moultonborough Public Library

Moultonborough Public Library, P. O. Box 150, Moultonborough 03254, Tele-
phone 476-8895.
Hours: Mon. & Wed. 1;30-8, Fri. 1:30-5, Sat. 10:30-4.
Holdings: Correspondence file of local families. Scrapbook collection.
Vital statistic file. Some town records includes holdings of Moulton-
borough Historical Society.

OSSIPEE (1785)

P. O. Box 67, Center Ossipee 03814, Telephone 539-4181.
Previous names: New Garden, Ossipee Gore, Wigwam Village.

Ossipee Historical Society, P. O. Box 245, Ossipee 03864, no telephone.
Hours: July-August Tues. & Thur. 10-2 and by appointment.
Holdings: Cemetery Lists. Some family papers. Business records. File of
local newspaper, CARROLL COUNTY INDEPENDENT.
Publications: OSSIPEE ALMANAC (quarterly newsletter, $6 annual membership).

Ossipee Public Library, Box 638, Main St., Center Ossipee 03814, Telephone
539-6390.
Hours: Mon. 6-8, Tues. & Wed. 10-8, Fri, & Sat. 10-2.
Holdings: Small book collection. Vertical file. File of two local newspapers, (Ossipee) TIMES and CARROLL COUNTY INDEPENDENT.

SANDWICH (1763)

P. O. Box 194, Center Sandwich 03227, Telephone 284-7113.

Samuel H. Wentworth Library, P. O. Box 146, Center Sandwich 03227, Telephone 284-6665.
Hours: Mon. 2-6, Wed. 2-8, Fri. 9-5, Sat, 9-1.
Holdings: Book collection. Name index for book collection. Micro film of
local census record. Some town records. File of vital statistics.File of
defunct local newspaper, SANDWICH REPORTER.

Sandwich Historical Society Museum, Box 106, Center Sandwich 03227, Telephone 284-6269.
Hours: July 4th-September 3rd, Mon-Sat. 11-5. May 28th - July 2d & Sept-
ember 5th - October 1st, Mon.- Fri. 2-5.
Holdings: Militia records. Some church, school, and town records. Some
files on local family.

TAMWORTH (1766)

P. O. Box 279, Tamworth 03886, Telephone 323-7971.

Chocorua Public Library, Chocorua 03817, Telephone 323-8610.
Hours: Mon. 6-9, Thur. 1-6, Sat. 1-5.
Holdings: Small book collection.

Cook Memorial Library, Main St., Tamworth 03886, Telephone 323-8510.
Hours: Tues. 10-12 & 7-9, Wed. 1:30-5 & 7-9, Sat. 1:15-4:45.
Holdings: Files on local families. Card file index on vital statistics.
Small book collection.

Tamworth Historical Society, P. O. Box 13, Tamworth 03886, no telephone.
Hours: By appt.
Holdings: Small book collection. Collection of unpublished manuscripts on
local genealogy.

TUFTONBORO (1795)
P. O. Box 98, Center Tuftonboro 03816, Telephone 569-4539.

Tuftonboro Free Library, Rt. 109A, Center Tuftonboro 03816, telephone
569-4256.
Hours: Tues. 2-8, Wed. & Thur. 2-5, Fri. 10-5.
Holdings: Small book collection. Some town records. Vertical file.

Tuftonboro Historical Society, P. O. Box 372, Melvin Village 03850, no tele-
phone.
Hours: By appt.
Holdings: Collection of records of local groups. A few family files.

WAKEFIELD (1774)
P. O. Box 279, Sanbornville 03872, Telephone 522-3327.
Previous names: East-town, Ham'-town, Watertown.

Wakefield-Brookfield Historical Society, P. O. Box 795, Sanbornville 03872,
no telephone.
Hours: By appt.
Holdings: Cemetery lists.

WOLFEBORO (1759)
South Main St., Box 1207, Wolfeboro 03894, Telephone 569-5328.
Previous names: Kingswood.

Wolfeboro Historical Society, P. O. Box 1066, Wolfeboro 03894, no telephone.
Hours: By appt.
Holdings: Clark family papers. Records of Pleasant Valley School.

Wolfeboro Public Library, Box 710, Wolfeboro 03894, Telephone 569-2428.
Hours: Mon., Tues. & Thur. 10-8, Wed. & Fri. 10-5:30, Sat. 10-3.
Holdings: Microfilm file of local newspaper, GRANITE STATE NEWS. Small
book collection. Some town records.

CHESHIRE COUNTY

Registrar of Deeds
33 West St.
Keene 03431.
Telephone 352-0403

Registrar of Probate
12 Court St.
Keene 03431-3499
Telephone 357-7786

ALSTEAD (1763)
P. O. Box 65, Alstead 03602, Telephone 835-2242.
Previous names: Alsted, Newton, No.#4.

Alstead Historical Society, Alstead 03602, no telephone.
Hours: By appt.
Holdings: Cemetery lists. Family papers, especially of the Walker and Still families. Records of local Universalist and Congregationalist churches.

Shedd-Porter Memorial Library, Main St., P. O. Box 87, Alstead 03602, Telephone 835-6661.
Hours: Winter: Wed. 12-4 & 6-8, Thur. & Fri. 12-6. Summer: Mon. & Fri. 12-6, Wed. 12-4 & 6-8.
Holdings: Some school and town records. Cemetery records. Files on local families,especially the Shedd and Ellis families.

CHESTERFIELD (1752)
P. O. Box 56, Chesterfield 03443, Telephone 363-8071.
Previous names: No. #1.

Chesterfield Historical Society, P. O. Box 204, Chesterfield 03443, no telephone.
Hours: By appt.
Holdings: Town records. Files on fifty local families.

Chesterfield Public Library, Main St., P. O. Box 158, Chesterfield 03443, Telephone 363-4621.
Hours: Mon. 10-3, Tues. 3-8, Thur. 10-8, Sat. 10-12.
Holdings: Cemetery lists.

DUBLIN (1749)
Box 62, Dublin 03444, Telephone 563-8859.
Previous names: Monadnock #3, North Monadnock.

Dublin Historical Society, P. O. Box 415, Dublin 03444, no telephone.
Hours: By appt.
Holdings: Many family papers, especially of the Brush, Gowing, James, Lamb and Smith families. Scrapbook collection. Clipping file. Indexed computer files on local vital statistics. Small book collection. Local militia records. File of local newspaper, DUBLIN NEWS. Records of many groups including Dublin Associates, Esquimo Lodge, Women's Community Club, Dublin Riding and Walking Club, and Garden Club. Papers of Stonewall Faith.
Publications: newsletter (quarterly $6. annual membership). Other publications include PEN, BRUSH, CHISEL AND CLEF - DUBLIN'S HALCYON DAYS by Elizabeth Pool ($6.).

FITZWILLIAM (1773)
P. O. Box 504, Fitzwilliam 03447, Telephone 585-7791.
Previous names: Monadnock #4, Stoddardstown.

Fitzwilliam Historical Society, P.O.Box 87, Fitzwilliam 03447, no telephone.
Hours: By appt.
Holdings: Papers of the Blake and White families. Large collection of 19th century business records and local deeds.
Publications: BLAKE HOUSE BULLENTIN (quarterly $6. annual membership).

Fitzwilliam Town Library, Village Common, Fitzwilliam 03447, Telephone 585-6503.
Hours: Mon. 2-5 & 6-8, Tues. & Thur. 2-5, Wed. 9-12, 2-5 & 6-8, Sat. 9-12.
Holdings: Some town records.

GILSUM (1763)
P. O. Box 36, Gilsum 03448, Telephone 357-0320.
Previous names: Boyle.

Gilsum Historical Society, P. O. Box 205, Gilsum 03448, no telephone.
Hours: By appt.
Holdings: Cemetery lists. Large collection of notes on local families.

Gilsum Public Library, P. O. Box 57, Gilsum 03448, Telephone 357-0320.
Hours: Mon. 1:30-3:30, Tues. & Wed. 1:30-3:30 & 6-8, Sat. 10-12.
Holdings: Cemetery lists. Some town records. Clipping file. Diary
collection. Vital statistics lists.

HARRISVILLE (1870)
P. O. Box 250, Harrisville 03450, Telephone 827-3431.
Previous names: Twitchellville.

Historic Harrisville, Inc., Church Hill, Harrisville 03450, Telephone
827-3722.
Hours: By appt.
Holdings: Colony family papers. Clipping file.

HINSDALE (1753)
R.R. 2, Box 125, Hinsdale 03451, Telephone 336-5820.
Previous names: Ft. Dummer.

Hinsdale Historical Society, Hinsdale 03451, no telephone.
Hours: By appt.
Holdings: Town records. Files of local defunct newspapers. Scrapbook col-
lection.

Hinsdale Public Library, P. O. Box 6, Hinsdale 03451, Telephone 336-5713.
Hours: Mon., Wed. through Fri. 2-5 & 6:30 to 8, Sat. 9-11:30. (No Saturday
hours in summer)
Holdings: Small book collection.

JAFFREY (1736)
69 Main St., Jaffrey 03452, Telephone 532-8322.
Previous names: Middle Monadnock, Middletown, Monadnock #2, Rowley Canada.

Jaffrey Historical Society, Civic Center, Jaffrey 03452, no telephone.
Hours: By appt.
Holdings: Small book collection. Several files of local newspapers.

Jaffrey Public Library, 111 Main St., Jaffrey 03452-1196, Telephone 532-7756
Hours: Mon., Wed., Fri. 11-5:30, Tues. & Thur. 1-8, Sat. 9-1.
Holdings: Small book collection. Collection of notes on French Canadian
families. Vital statistic lists. Some church records. Some town records.
Files of several local newspapers including JAFFREY REPORTER and MONADNOCK
BREEZE.

*KEENE (1735)
3 Washington St., Keene 03431, Telephone 352-0133.
Previous names: Keeneborough, Upper Ashuelot.

Historical Society of Cheshire County, P. O. Box 803, Keene 03431, Telephone
352-1895.
Hours: Mon. through Fri. 9-4.
Holdings: Files of fifty Cheshire county newspapers including the defunct
CHESHIRE REPUBLICAN and NEW HAMPSHIRE SENTINEL. Keene municipal records.
Papers of the Eliot family. Files on fifty families. Seventy-five files
of town, school, and church records from the Cheshire county area. Large
collection of Civil War era diaries and letters.
PUBLICATIONS: newsletter (five times per year, $15. annual membership).
Other publications include VERY POOR AND OF A LOW MAKE: THE DIARY OF ALAN
SANGER ($30.).

Keene Public Library, 60 Winter St., Keene 03431, Telephone 352-0157.
Hours: Mon. through Thur. 10-9, Fri. 10-6, Sat. 9-5.
Holdings: Large book collection. Vertical file. File of local newspaper
KEENE SENTINEL.

Special Collection, Mason Library, Keene State College, Keene 03431.

Telephone 352-1909, ext. 237.
Hours: Mon. through Thur. 8-11, Fri. 8-5, Sat. 10-5, Sun. 2-11.
Holdings: Large collection of pre-Revolutionary War property records. Some
papers of the Eliot family.

MARLBOROUGH (1752)

P. O. Box 515, Marlborough 03455, Telephone 876-4529.
Previous names: Monadnock #5, New Marlborough, Oxford.

Frost Free Library, P. O. Box 416, Marlborough 03455, Telephone 876-4479.
Hours: Winter: Tues. & Wed. 2-8, Thur. through Sat. 2-5, Summer: Tues. &
Wed. 2-8, Thur. 10-5, Fri. & Sat. 2-5.
Holdings: Holdings of Marlborough Historical Society (Clipping file, corres-
pondence files on local families, some town and school records).

Marlborough Historical Society-See Frost Free Library.

MARLOW (1753)

P. O. Box 255, Marlow 03456, Telephone 446-2245.
Previous names: Addison.

Marlow Historical Society, Marlow 03456, no telephone.
Hours: By appt.
Holdings: Records of local GAR post. Phelps family papers. Several files
of area newspapers. Collection of local Free-Will Baptist and Universalist
publications. Small book collection.

PC Connections, 6 Mill St., Marlow 03456, Telephone 446-3383, ext. 3130.
Hours: Mon. through Fri. 9-5.
Holdings: Files on five hundred families. Census records up to 1920. Files
on local homes. Notebook collection on genealogy of Civil War veterans.
The company is funding the acquisition and cataloging of historic records
for the Marlow Historical Society and is acting as a repository until the
society acquires adequate facilities.

NELSON (1752)

P. O. Box 60, Munsonville 03457, Telephone 847-9043.
Previous names: Monadnock #6, Packersfield.

Olivia Rodham Memorial Library, RFD, Marlborough 03455, Telephone 847-3214.
Hours: Mon. 12:30-4:30, Wed. 6:30-9, Fri. 6-8:30, Sat. 9-12.
Holdings: Some town records. Small book collection.

RICHMOND (1735)

229 Lang Rd., Richmond 03470, Telephone 239-4232.
Previous names: Sylvester Canada.

Richmond Archives, 480 Fitzwilliam Rd., Richmond 03470, no telephone.
Hours: By appt.
Holdings: Notes and papers of late local historian Roger Hunt. Small collection of published and unpublished genealogies. Town records. The Archives is a joint facility of the town and Richmond Historical Society.

Richmond Public Library, 19 Winchester., Richmond 03470, Telephone
239-6164.
Hours: Winter: Tues. 1-8, Sat. 1-5. Summer: Tues. 2-8, Sat. 9-1.
Holdings: Some town records.

RINDGE (1736)

P. O. Box 11, Rindge 03461, Telephone 899-3354.
Previous names: Monadnock #1, Rowley-Canada, South Monadnock, South Merrimack.

DiPrieto Library, Franklin Pierce College, College Road, P. O. Box 60,
Rindge 03461, Telephone 899-5111.

Hours: Mon. through Sat. 8-4.
Holdings: Large collection of town histories from southwestern New Hampshire

Ingalls Memorial Library, Main St., Box 224, Rindge 03461, Telephone
899-3303.
Hours: Mon. 1:30-5:30 and 7-9, Tues. 5-9, Wed. & Fri. 1:30-5:30, Thur.
10:30- 5:30, Sat. 9-12.
Holdings: Small book collection. Some town records.

Rindge Historical Society, Rindge 03461, no telephone.
Hours: By appt.
Holdings: Computerized cemetery lists. Todd family papers. Wood family
diaries. Town records. Some local newspaper files.

ROXBURY (1812)
RFD 4, Box 236, Roxbury 03431, Telephone 352-4903.

STODDARD (1752)
Rt. 9, Box 532, Stoddard 03464, Telephone 446-2203.
Previous names: Limerick, Monadnock #7.

Davis Public Library, Rt. 123, Stoddard 03464, no telephone.
Hours: Winter: Wed. 9-10, Thur. 7-9, Summer: Thur. 7-9, Sat. 9-10.
Holdings: Small book collection.

Stoddard Historical Society, HCR 32, Box 551, Stoddard 03464, no telephone.
Hours: By appt.
Holdings: Papers and notes of late local historian Charles L. Pierce. Town
records.

SULLIVAN (1787)
HCR 33, Box 228, Keene 03431, Telephone 352-1495.

Sullivan Public Library, P. O. Box 92, Sullivan 03445, Telephone 847-3458.
Hours: Tues. 10-12, and every other Sun. 1-4.
Holdings: Scrapbook collection.

SURRY (1769)
78 Village Rd., Surry 03431, Telephone 352-2000.
Previous names: Westmorland Leg.

Reed Free Library, HCR 32, Box 43, Keene 03431, Telephone 352-1761.
Hours: Winter: Mon. & Thur. 3-8, Summer: Mon. & Thur. 4-9.
Holdings: Small book collection. Some town records.

SWANZEY (1733)
P. O. Box 9, East Swanzey 03446, Telephone 352-7411.
Previous names: Lower Ashuelot.

Mt. Caesar Union Library, P. O. Box 8, Swanzey Center, East Swanzey 03446,
Telephone 357-0456.
Hours: Mon. & Wed. 1-5 and 6:30-9, Tues. & Thur. 9:30-11:30, 1-5 and 6:30-
9.
Holdings: Small book collection.

Stratton Free Library, P. O. Box 578, West Swanzey 03469, Telephone
352-9391.
Hours: Tues. 2:30-8, Thur. 2:30-6, Sat. 11-2.
Holdings: Small book collection. Vertical file.

Swanzey Historical Museum, P. O. Box 416, West Swanzey 03469, Telephone
352-4579.
Hours: By appt.

Holdings: Correspondence file on local families. Oral history tape collection.

TROY (1815)
P. O. Box 249, Troy 03465, Telephone 242-3845.

Gay-Kimball Public Library, P. O. Box 837, Troy 03465, Telephone 242-7743.
Hours: Tue. through Thur. 1:30-7:30, Sat. 11-3.
Holdings: Small book collection. Some town records.

WALPOLE (1752)
P. O. Box 756, Walpole 03608, Telephone 756-3514.
Previous names: Bellowstown, Great Falls, Lunenburg, No. #3.

Walpole Historical Society, P. O. Box 305, Walpole 03608, Telephone 756-3449
Hours: June-Sept. Sat. & Sun. and by Appt.
Holdings: Bellows and Hubbard family papers. Some town records. Clipping
file. Business records. Oral history tape collection. File of several
local defunct newspapers including the WALPOLE GAZETTE.

Walpole Town Library, P. O. Box 487, Main St., Walpole 03608, Telephone
756-9806.
Hours: Mon. 2-5 & 7-9, Tues. through Fri. 2-5, Sat. 9-12 & 2-4.
Holdings: Small book collection.

WESTMORELAND (1735)
Town Hall, Westmoreland 03467, Telephone 399-4471.
Previous names: Great Meadows, Line of Town #2.

Westmoreland Historical Society-see Westmoreland Public Library.

Westmoreland Public Library, South Village Rd., Westmoreland 03467, Telephone 399-7750.
Hours: Monday 9-12 and 5-8, Thur. 1-6, Sat. 9-1.
Holdings: Large collection of local diaries. Correspondence files on local
families especially the Hutchins and Noyes families. Includes holdings of
Westmoreland Historical Society.

WINCHESTER (1733)
1 Richmond St., Winchester 03470, Telephone 239-6233.
Previous names: Arlington, Earlington.

Conant Public Library, P. O. Box 6, Winchester 03470, Telephone 239-4331,
Hours: Winter: Mon., Wed., Fri. 10-8. Summer: Mon. & Wed. 10-8. Fri 10-5
(July-Oct.) Sat. 9-12 (July-Oct.)..
Holdings: Large book collection on local history. Town records on microfilm
Local newspaper on file WINCHESTER STAR.

COOS COUNTY

Registrar of Deeds
Lancaster 03584
Telephone 788-2392

Registrar of Probate
148 Main St.
Lancaster 03584-0306
Telephone 788-2001

*BERLIN (1771)
City Hall, Main St., Berlin 03570, Telephone 752-2340.
Previous names: Maynesborough.

Berlin Historical Society, P. O. Box 52, Berlin 03570, no telephone.
Hours: By appt.

Holdings: Several thousand genealogy data sheets from Coos County families.

Berlin Public Library, 270 Main St., Berlin 03570, Telephone 752-5210.
Hours: Mon. through Fri. 10-9.
Holdings: Many local church records. File of local newspaper BERLIN
REPORTER. Municipal records. Complete set of city directories.

CARROLL (1772)
P. O. Box 88, Twin Mountain 03595, Telephone 846-5494.
Previous names: Bretton Wood.

CLARKSVILLE (1853)
RFD 1, Box 460, Pittsburg 03592, Telephone 246-7751.
Previous names: Dartmouth College Grant.

COLEBROOK (1762)
10 Bridge St., Colebrook 03576, Telephone 237-4070.
Previous names: Dryden.

Colebrook Public Library, P. O. Box 58, Main St., Colebrook 03576, Telephone
237-4808.
Hours: Mon. through Thur. 2-5:30, Fri. 10-5:30, Sat. 10-12.
Holdings: Small book collection. Some town records. File of local newspaper (Colebrook) NEWS & SENTINEL.

COLUMBIA (1762)
RR 1, Box 523, Colebrook 03576, Telephone 237-5255.
Previous names: Cockburne, Cockburntown, Preston.

DALTON (1764)
RFD 2, Box 143, Whitefield 03598, Telephone 837-9802.
Previous names: Apthorp, Chiswick.

Dalton Historical Society-see Dalton Public Library.

Dalton Public Library, RR 2, Box 144, Whitefield 03598-9305, Telephone
837-2751.
Hours: Mon. 2-5, Wed. 2-5 & 6:30 to 8:30, Sat. 10-12.
Holdings: Some town records. Holdings of the Dalton Historical Society
(correspondence file on local families, scrapbook collection).

DIXVILLE (1805)
Dixville Notch 03576, Telephone 255-3791.

DUMMER (1848)
RFD 1, Box 285, Milan 03588, Telephone 449-3408.

ERROL (1774)
P. O. Box 74, Errol 03579, Telephone 482-3351.

GORHAM (1836)
20 Park St., Gorham 03581, Telephone 466-2744.
Previous Names: Shelburne Addition.

Gorham Historical Society, 25 Railroad St., Gorham 03581, no telephone.
Hours: By appt.
Holdings: Some town and school records. Few files on local families.

Gorham Public Library, 20 Park St., Gorham 03581, Telephone 466-2525.
Hours: Mon. through Fri. 1-9.
Holdings: Some town records. Vertical file.

Mount Washington Observatory, 1 Washington St., Gorham 03581, Telephone
356-8345.

Hours: Thur. 9-5.
Holdings: Complete file of local newspaper AMONG THE CLOUDS.

JEFFERSON (1765)
RFD 1, Box 162A, Jefferson 03583, Telephone 586-4553.
Previous names: Dartmouth.

Jefferson Historical Society, RR 1, Box 5A-1, Jefferson 03583, no telephone.
Hours: by appt.
Holdings: Manuscript collection on local families especially the Rines family.

LANCASTER (1763)
P. O. Box 151, Lancaster 03584, Telephone 788-2306.
Previous names: Upper Coos.

Lancaster Historical Society, P. O. Box 473, Lancaster 03584, no telephone.
Hours: By appt.
Holdings: Cemetery lists. Some files of family papers. Records of the
First Church of Lancaster. Vital statistics list. Small collection of genealogies. Correspondence file on local families.

Weeks Memorial Library, Box 350, Lancaster 03584, Telephone 788-3352.
Hours: Mon., Wed., Fri. 1-4:30 and 7-9, Sat. 10-12.
Holdings: Large book collection. Some town records. File of area newspaper.COOS COUNTY DEMOCRAT.

MILAN (1771)
P. O. Box 158, Milan 03588, Telephone 449-3461.
Previous names: Paulsbourg.

MILLSFIELD (1932)
P. O. Box 48, Errol 03579, no telephone.

NORTHUMBERLAND (1761)
2 State St., Groveton 03582, Telephone 636-1451.
Previous names: Groveton, Stonington.

Norththumberland Public Library, P. O. Box 64, State St., Groveton 03582,
Telephone 636-2066.
Hours: Mon. through Wed. 12-4 & 6-8, Thur. & Fri. 9:30-4.
Holdings: Some census records. Some town records. Cemetery records.

PITTSBURG (1840)
P. O. Box 127, Pittsburg 03592, Telephone 538-6697.
Previous names: Indian Stream Territory.

Pittsburg Historical Society, P. O. Box 128, Pittsburg 03592, no telephone.
Hours: By appt.
Holdings: Baldwin family papers. Vertical file. Clipping file. File on
local families. Cemetery lists.

RANDOLPH (1772)
RD 1, Timberglade, Box 139, Jefferson 03583, Telephone 466-5771.
Previous name: Durand.

SHELBURNE (1769)
Philbrook Farm Inn, Shelburne 03581, Telephone 466-3831.

Shelburne Public Library, Star Rte. 51, Gorham 03581, Telephone 466-3986.
Hours: Thur. 2-4, Sat. 10-1.
Holdings: Small book collection.

STARK (1774)

RFD 1, Box 379, Groveton 03582, Telephone 636-2118.
Previous names: General John Winslow Grant, Percy, Piercy.

STEWARTSTOWN (1770)
P. O. Box 35, West Stewartstown 03597, Telephone 246-3329.
Previous names: Stuart, Stuartstown.

STRATFORD (1762)
P. O. Box 366, North Stratford 03590, Telephone 922-5598.
Previous names: Woodbury.

Stratford Public Library, P. O. Box 193, North Stratford 03590, no telephone.
Hours: Tues. 1-3, Sat. 2-4.
Holdings: Some town records.

WHITEFIELD (1774)
7 Jefferson Rd., Whitefield 03598, Telephone 837-9871.

Whitefield Historical Society, Whitefield 03598, no telephone.
Hours; By appt.
Holdings: Town records. Files on local families. Some newspaper files.

Whitefield Public Library, 12 High St., Whitefield 03598, Telephone 837-2030.
Hours: Mon. 9-12 & 5-8, Tues. & Thur. 2-8, Sat. 10-5.
Holdings: Some town records. Some newspaper files.

GRAFTON COUNTY

Registrar of Deeds
Court House
North Haverhill 03774
Telephone 787-6921

Registrar of Probate
P. O. Box 206
Woodsville 03785
Telephone 787-6931

ALEXANDRIA (1753)
RFD 1, Box 807, Alexandria 03217, Telephone 744-3220.

Haynes Memorial Library, RFD 1, Box 833, Bristol 03222, no telephone.
Hours: Mon. 1:30-4:30 & 7-8.
Holdings: Town records. Small book collection.

ASHLAND (1868)
P. O. Box 32, Ashland 03217, Telephone 968-4432.

Ashland Historical Society, 20 School St., Ashland 03217, no telephone.
Hours: By appt.
Holdings: Whipple family papers.

BATH (1760)
P. O. Box 165, Bath 03740, Telephone 747-2454.
Previous names: No. #10.

BENTON (1764)
RFD 2, Box 348, Woodsville 03785, Telephone 787-6541.
Previous names: Coventry.

BETHLEHEM (1799)
Main St., Town Bldg., Bethlehem 03574, Telephone 869-2293.
Previous names: Lloyd's Hill.

Bethlehem Public Library, P. O. Box 250, Main St, Bethlehem 03574-0250,
Telephone 869-2409.
Hours: Mon. through Fri. 1-4:30, Mon. & Thur. 6:30-9.
Holdings: Some town records.

BRIDGEWATER (1788)
RFD 2, Plymouth 03264, Telephone 968-7911.

Bridgewater Historical Society-see Bridgewater Public Library.

Bridgewater Public Library, RFD 2, Box 389, Plymouth 03264, Telephone
968-7911.
Hours: Mon.& Wed. 6:8:30 First and third Sat. of each month 1-3.
Holdings: Small book collection. Some town records. Cemetery records.
Voting lists. Files on local families especially the Hammer family.

BRISTOL (1819)
P. O. Box 297, Bristol 03222, Telephone 744-8478.

Bristol Historical Society, Box 400, Bristol 03222, no telephone.
Hours: By appt.
Holdings: Cemetery lists. Partial file of defunct local newspapers.

Minot-Sleeper Library, Pleasant St., Bristol 03222, Telephone 744-3352.
Hours: Mon. & Wed. 1-8, Fri. 3-8, Sat. 9-12.
Holdings: Some town records. Large book collection. File of local news-
paper BRISTOL ENTERPRISE.

CAMPTON (1761)
P. O. Box 296, Campton 03223, Telephone 726-3223.

Campton Historical Society, Campton 03223, no telephone.
Hours: By appt.
Holdings: Small book collection. Dole family papers.

CANAAN (1761)
P. O. Box 38, Canaan 03741-0038, Telephone 523-7106.

Canaan Historical Museum Society, Elmhurst, RR 1, Box 81, Canaan 03741, no
telephone.
Hours: By appt.
Holdings: Many files of local defunct newspapers.

DORCHESTER (1761)
RFD 1, Box 490, Rumney 03266, Telephone 786-9476.

EASTON (1867)
381 Easton Valley Rd., Easton 03580, Telephone 823-5293.
Previous names: Eastern Landaff.

Easton Public Library, RFD 1, Franconia 03580, no telephone.
Hours: First and Third Wed. of each month 3-5:30.
Holdings: Some town records.

ELLSWORTH (1769)
RFD 1, Box 853, Plymouth 03264, Telephone 726-4748.
Previous names: Trecothick.

ENFIELD (1761)
P. O. Box 373, Enfield 03748, Telephone 632-5001.
Previous names: Endfield, Relhan.

Town of Enfield Historical Records, P. O. Box 373, Enfield 03748, no tele-
field.
Hours: By appt.

Holdings: Joint facility of the Enfield Public Library, Town of Enfield and
Enfield Historical Society. Vertical file. Town records. Shaker history
collection. Scrapbook collection. Obituary notice file. Correspondence
file on local families. Nichols family papers. Microfilm files of three
newspapers VALLEY NEWS, HOMETOWN MESSENGER, MASCOMA MESSENGER.

FRANCONIA (1764)
P. O. Box 900, Franconia 03580, Telephone 823-7752.
Previous names: Indian Head, Morristown,.

Abbie Greenleaf Library, Box 130, Franconia 03580, Telephone 823-8424.
Hours: Winter: Mon. through Wed. 2-5, Thur. 10-12 & 2-5, Fri. 2-5, Sat. 10-
12. Summer: Mon. & Tues. 2-6, Wed. 2-8, Thur. 10-12 & 2-5, Fri. 2-5, Sat.
10-12.
Holdings: Small book collection.

GRAFTON (1761)
P. O. Box 277, Grafton 03240, Telephone 523-7700.

Grafton Public Library, Library Road, Grafton 03240, no telephone.
Hours: Wed. 3-5 & 6:30-8.
Holdings: Some town records. Small book collection.

GROTON (1761)
P. O. Box 395, Hebron 03241, Telephone 744-8849.
Previous names: Cockermouth.

HANOVER (1761)
P. O. Box 483, Hanover 03755, Telephone 643-4123.
Previous names: Dresden.

Archives, Baker Library, Dartmouth College, Hanover 03755, Telephone
646-2235.
Hours: Mon. through Fri. 9-4:30.
Holdings: Cemetery records for fourteen New Hampshire towns. Hanover town
records. Papers of 145 families (which includes many town and other government records) including the Dow, Bean, Clark, Freeman, Mathewson, Morton,
Riddle, Sanborn, Wheelock, Woodbury and Tuck families. Numerous church records. Has on file 100 newspapers. Computer survey of location of individual copies of all pre-1900 New Hampshire newspapers in the state. Includes
holdings of Hanover Historical Society.
Publications: A GUIDE TO GENEALOGICAL RESEARCH IN THE DARTMOUTH COLLEGE
LIBRARY By Robert D. Jaccand ($6).

Hanover Historical Society-see Archives, Baker Library, Dartmouth College.

HAVERHILL (1763)
Court St., Woodsville 03785, Telephone 747-2808.
Previous names: Lower Coos.

Haverhill Historical Society-see Haverhill Library Association.

Haverhill Library Association, P. O. Box 117, Court St., Haverhill 03765,
Telephone 989-5578.
Hours: Wed. 2-5 & 6-9, Sat. 10-2.
Holdings: Holdings of the Haverhill Historical Society (notes and papers of
late local historian Frank Rogers, Westgate family papers).

North Haverhill Library, Box 55, North Haverhill 03744, no telephone.
Hours: Mon. 6:30-8, Wed. 1-4 & 6:30-8.
Holdings: Small book collection.

Woodsville Free Public Library, 14 School St., Woodsville 03785, Telephone
747-3483.

Hours: Mon., Wed., Fri. 1-8.
Holdings: Small book collection. Clipping file.

HEBRON (1792)
Star Rt., Box 286, East Hebron 03232, Telephone 744-2631.

Hebron Historical Society, P. O. Box 89, Hebron 03241, no telephone.
Hours: By appt.
Holdings: Files on local families.especially the Bal family.

HOLDERNESS (1751)
P. O. Box 203, Holderness 03245, Telephone 968-7536.
Previous names: New Holderness.

Holderness Free Library, P. O. Box L, Holderness 03245, Telephone 968-7066
Hours: Mon., Wed., Sat. 10-6, Fri. 2-8.
Holdings: Some town records, Vertical file. Files on local families. Cemetery lists. Includes holdings of Holderness Historical Society.

Holderness Historical Society-see Holderness Free Library.

LANDAFF (1769)
160 Landaff Rd., Lisbon 03585, Telephone 838-6220.
Previous names: Witcherville.

*LEBANON (1761)
51 North Park St., Lebanon 03766, Telephone 448-3054.

Lebanon Historical Society, 40 Mascoma St., Lebanon 03766, no telephone.
Hours: By appt.
Holdings: Carter family papers. 900 files on local families. Some business records.

Lebanon Public Library, 9 East Park St., Lebanon 03766, Telephone 448-2459.
Hours: Mon. through Fri. 10-5 & 7-9, Sat. 10-5.
Holdings: Files on local families, especially the Alden family. Microfilm collection of Colonial era deeds. Files of two newspapers, VALLEY NEWS AND GRANITE STATE FREE PRESS.

LINCOLN (1764)
Main St., Lincoln 03251, Telephone 745-8971.
Previous names: Henryville, Pullman.

Lincoln Public Library, Box 98, Lincoln 03251, Telephone 745-8159.
Hours: Mon. through Wed. 12-5 & 7-9, Sat. 7-9.
Holdings: Some town records.

LISBON (1763)
P. O. Box 222, Lisbon 03585, Telephone 838-2862.
Previous names: Chiswick, Concord, Gunthwaite.

Lisbon Historical Society-see Lisbon Public Library.

Lisbon Public Library, 22 School St., Lisbon 03585-1397, Telephone 838-5506.
Hours: Mon., Wed. & Fri. 11-5 & 6:30-8:30.
Holdings: Holdings of Lisbon Historical Society (town records, cemetery records, papers of some local families).

LITTLETON (1770)
1 Union St., Littleton 03561, Telephone 444-3995.
Previous names: Pettenville.

Littleton Area Historical Society, 4 Merrill St., Littleton 03561, no telephone.

19

Hours: By appt.
Holdings: Kilburn family papers. Town records. Book collection. Vital statistics list.

Littleton Public Library, School St., Littleton 03561, Telephone 444-5601.
Hours: Tues., Thur. & Fri. 9-5, Wed. 9:30-8, Sat. 9:30-12.
Holdings: Some town records. Small book collection. Microfilm file of local newspaper, LITTLETON COURIER and several defunct newspapers.

LYMAN (1761)
RFD 1, Box 507B, Lisbon 03585, Telephone 838-6113.

LYME (1761)
RR 1, Box 153, Lyme 02768, Tleephone 795-4416.

Converse Free Library, RR 1, Box 1, Lyme 03768, Telephone 795-4622.
Hours: Mon. 1-6, Tues. & Thur. 9-5, Wed. 9-9, Sat. 10-5.
Holdings: Small book collection. Some town records.

Lyme Historians, Lyme Historical Museum, Lyme 03768, no telephone.
Hours: By appt.
Holdings: Scrapbook collection. Vertical file.

MONROE (1854)
RR 1, Box 326, Monroe 03771, Telephone 638-2644.
Previous names: Hurd.

ORANGE (1769)
RFD 2, Box 185, Canaan 03741, no telephone.
Previous names: Bradford, Cardigan, Liscomb, Middletown.

Orange Historical Commission, Orange town hall, RFD 2, Box 185, Canaan 03741, no telephone.
Hours: By appt.
Holdings: Town records.

ORFORD (1761)
RR Box 10, Orford 03777, Telephone 353-4858.
Previous names: No. #7, Sugar River.

Orford Free Library, RR1, Box 155, Brook Rd., Orfordville, Orford 03777, Telephone 353-9166.
Hours: Tues. 12:30-7, Fri. 12:30-5,.
Holdings: Some town records. Small collection of family papers. Vertical file.

Orford Social Library, Box 189, Orford 03777, Telephone 353-9756.
Hours: Thur. 5-7, Fri. 2-5, Sat. 11-1.
Holdings: Files of many families especially the Marston, Mann and Morey family. Small book collection.

Piermont (1764)
RR2, Box 244A, Pike 03780, Telephone 272-4840.

Piermont Historical Society, P. O. Box 58, Piermont 03779, no telephone.
Hours: By appt.
Holdings: Town and school records.

Piermont Public Library, P. O. Box 6, Piermont 03779, Telephone 272-4967.
Hours: Tues. 10-8, Thur. 5-8, Sun. 3-5 (only in October, November, January, February).
Holdings: Small book collection. Some town records. Clipping file.

PLYMOUTH (1763)

Court House, Main St., Plymouth 03264, Telephone 536-1732.
Previous names: New Plymouth.

Herbert H. Lanson Library, Plymouth 'State College, Plymouth 03264, Telephone 536-1550, ext. 257.
Hours: Mon. through Fri. 8-5.
Holdings: Large oral history tape collection. Small book collection on local families. Records of the Institute of New Hampshire Studies.

Institute of New Hampshire Studies-see Herbert H. Lanson Library.

Pease Public Library, 1 Russell St., Plymouth 03264-1414, Telephone 536-2616.
Hours: Winter: Mon. & Wed. 12-9, Fri. 10-8 (Oct.-May) Sat. 10-3(losed July-Aug.). Summer: Mon. & Wed. 12-9, Fri. 10-9 (June-Sept.).
Holdings: Some town records. Small book collection.

Plymouth Historical Society, 1 Court St., Plymouth 03264, Telephone 536-2337.
Hours: May-Dec. Wed. 3-8 & Sat. 11-4 and by appt.
Holdings: Papers and notes of late local historian George Clarke. Town records. Cemetery lists. Scattered runs of defunct local newspapers.

RUMNEY (1761)
Box 119A, Rumney 03266, no telephone.

Byron G. Merrill Library, Rumney 03266, Telephone 786-9520.
Hours: Tues. & Thur. 2-5 & 6:30-8:30, Sat. 10-12.
Holdings: Some town records. Cemetery lists. Small collection of genealogies.

SUGAR HILL (1962)
Box 574, Sugar Hill 03585, Telephone 823-8468.

Sugar Hill Historical Museum, P. O. Box 654, Sugar Hill 03585, no telephone.
Hours: By appt.
Holdings: Records of 100 local families dating from 1787.

THORNTON (1763)
Box 830B, Thornton 03223, Telephone 726-4232.
Previous names: Blanchard's Gore, Waterville Gore.

Thornton Public Library, RFD 1, Rt. 175, Thornton 03223, Telephone 726-8981.
Hours: Tues. 10-6, Wed. 10-5, Thur. 10-3, Fri. 10-5.
Holdings: Some town records.

WARREN (1764)
P. O. Box 40, Warren 03279, Telephone 764-5780.

Warren Historical Society, Box 35, Glencliff 03238, no telephone.
Hours: By appt.
Holdings: File of local newspaper, HAVERHILL RECORD. Notes of late local historian Nettie Brown. Town records. Hitchner family papers.

WATERVILLE VALLEY (1829)
Town office, Waterville Valley 03215, Telephone 236-4730.
Previous names: Gillis & Foss Grant, Waterville.

WENTWORTH (1766)
RR1, Box 439, Wentworth 03266, Telephone 764-5244.

WOODSTOCK (1763)
Box 156, North Woodstock 03262, Telephone 745-8752.
Previous names: Fairfield, Peeling.

Moosllauke Public Library, Woodstock Town Bldg., Lost River Rd., North
Woodstock 03262, Telephone 745-9971.
Hours: Mon. 10-7, Thur. & Sat. 9-5.
Holdings: Vertical file. Small book collection.

HILLSBOROUGH COUNTY

Registrar of Deeds
19 Temple St.
Nashua 03060
Telephone 882-6933

Registrar of Probate
P. O. Box P
19 Temple St.
Nashua 03061
Telephone 424-7844

AMHERST (1760)
P. O. Box 960, Amherst 03031, Telephone 673-6041.
Previous names: Narragansett #3, Salem Narragansett, Souhegan West.

Amherst Town Library, 14 Main St., Amherst 03031, Telephone 673-2288.
Hours: Mon. through Thur. 9:30-8:30, Fri. 9:30-5, Sat. 9:30-3:30 (9:30-12:30
in summer). Sun. 1-4 (summer only).
Holdings: Book collection on local families. Some town records. Papers of
the Sullivan, Shattuck, Melendy and Wilkins families. File of area newspaper MILFORD CABINET. Includes holdings of the Historical Society of Amherst

Historical Society of Amherst, see Amherst Town Library.

ANTRIM (1777)
P. O. Box 517, Antrim 03440, Telephone 588-6785.

Antrim Historical Society-see James A. Tuttle Library.

James A. Tuttle Library, Main St., Antrim 03440, Telephone 588-6786.
Hours: Mon. 2-5, Tues. 2-6, Thur. 2-8, Fri. 9-12, Sat. 10-4.
Holdings: Small book collection. Some town records. Includes holdings of
Antrim Historical Society (files on local families, cemetery lists, audio
tape collection on local history, collection of family bibles with genealog-
ies written in them).

BEDFORD (1730)
24 North Amherst Rd., Bedford 03110, Telephone 472-3550.

Bedford Historical Society, Town Office Blad., Bedford 03110, no telephone.
Hours: By appt.
Holdings: Large correspondence file on local families. Small collection of
local genealogies. Patton family papers.

Bedford Public Library, Meetinghouse Rd., Bedford 03110, Telephone 472-3023.
Hours: Mon. through Thur. 9-8, Fri. 9-5, Sat. 10-3 (no hours in July or Aug)
Sun. 12-2 (no hours in July or Aug.).
Holdings: File of local newspaper, BEDFORD-MERRIMACK BULLENTIN. Some town
records. Small book collection.

BENNINGTON (1842)
School St., Bennington 03442-0285, Telephone 588-2189.
Previous names: Hancock Factory Village.

Bennington Historical Society, P. O. Box 50, Bennington 03442, no telephone.
Hours: By appt.
Holdings: Files on local families.

G. E. P. Dodge Library, P. O. Box 307, Bennington 03442, Telephone 588-6585.
Hours: Mon. 9-6, Thur. 12-8, Fri. 12-5, Sun. 4-6. (no hours in summer).
Holdings: Vertical file.

BROOKLINE (1769)
P. O. Box 336, Brookline 03033, Telephone 673-8933.
Previous names: Brooklyne, Mile Slip.

Brookline Historical Society, 48 Mason Rd., Brookline 03073, no telephone.
Hours: By appt.
Holdings: Town records. School records. Small book collection.

DEERING (1774)
RD1, Box 62, Hillsborough 03244, Telephone 464-3248.
Previous names: Cumberland, Society Land.

Deering Historical Society-see Deering Public Library.

Deering Public Library, Box 236, RFD 1, Deering 03244, no telephone.
Hours: Winter: (at Town Hall) Wed. 11-12, Thur. 5-7. Summer: (at Library)
Wed. 10-12 & 1-3, Thur. 5-7.
Holdings: Large book collection. Some town records. Includes holdings of
the Deering Historical Society.

FRANCESTOWN (1772)
P. O. Box 118, Francestown 03580, Telephone 547-6251.
Previous names: Lyndeborough Addition, New Boston Addition.

Francestown Improvement and Historical Society, Main St., Francestown 03043,
no telephone.
Hours: By appointment.
Holdings: Woodbury family papers. File on every structure in town. Records of local soapstone mining industry. Records of Francestown Academy.
Publications: FRANCESTOWN (quarterly newsletter for $5. annual membership).

GOFFSTOWN (1748)
16 Main St., Goffstown 03045, Telephone 497-3613.
Previous names: Narragansett #4, Piscataquoq, Shove's Town.

Goffstown Historical Society, 19 Parker Station Rd., Goffstown 03045, no
telephone.
Hours: By appt.
Holdings: Small book collection. Large file on Kidder family.

Goffstown Public Library, 2 High St., Goffstown 03045, Telephone 497-2102.
Hours: Mon. & Wed. 10-8, Tues., Thur. & Fri. 10-6, Sat. 10-3 (no Sat. hours
in summer) Sun. 12-2 (no Sun. hours in summer).
Holdings: Small book collection, Some town records, File of local newspaper
GOFFSTOWN NEWS.

GREENFIELD (1791)
P. O. Box 16, Greenfield 03047, Telephone 547-2782.
Previous names: Lyndeborough Addition.

Greenfield Historical Society, P. O. Box 213, Greenfield 03047, no telephone
Hours: By appt.
Holdings: Files on families especially the Cragin family. Cemetery list.
Clipping file.

Stephenson Memorial Library, Box 127, Forest Rd., Greenfield 03047, Telephone 547-2790.
Hours: Mon. 12-5 & 6-8, Wed. & Fri. 12-6, Sat. 9-12.
Holdings: Small book collection. Some town records.

GREENVILLE (1872)
P. O. Box 354, Greenville 03048, Telephone 878-4155.
Previous names: Mason Harbor, Mason Village, Slipton.

Chamberlin Public Library, Box 499, Main St., Greenville 03048, Telephone
878-1105.
Hours: Mon. & Wed. 7-9, Tues. Thur. & Fri. 9:30-5, Sat. 9-1 (no Sat. hours
in July or Aug.).
Holdings: Small book collection. Some town records.

HANCOCK (1779)
P. O. Box 6, Hancock 03449, Telephone 525-4441.

HILLSBOROUGH (1735)
P. O. Box 1699, Hillsborough 03244, Telephone 464-5571.
Previous names: No. #7.

Hillsborough Historical Society, P. O. Box 896, Hillsborough 03244, no tele-
phone.
Hours: By appt.
Holdings: Pierce family papers.

HOLLIS (1746)
7 Monument Square, Hollis 03049, Telephone 465-2064.
Previous names: Nittisset, One Pine Grant, West Dunstable, West Parish
Dunstable.

Hollis Historical Society, P. O. Box 138, Hollis 03049, Telephone 456-7696.
Hours: By appt.
Holdings: Town records. Files on local families.

Hollis Social Library, P. O. Box 659, Hollis 03049, Telephone 465-7721.
Hours: Mon. & Wed. 1:30-5:30 & 7-9, Tues. & Fri. 1:30-5:30, Thur. 11-5:30,
Sat. 9-3.
Holdings: Small book collection. Some town records. Scrapbook collection.

HUDSON (1741)
12 School St., Hudson 03051, Telephone 886-6003.
Previous names: Nottingham, Nottingham West.

Hills Memorial Library, 18 Library St., Hudson 03051, Telephone 886-6030.
Hours: Mon. through Thur. 9:30-9, Fri. & Sat. 9:30-5 (no summer hours on
Sat.), Sun. 1-5 (no summer/spring hours on Sun.).
Holdings: Small book collection. Some town records. Vertical file.

Hudson Historical Society, Derry Rd., Hudson 03051, Telephone 882-4744.
Hours: By appt.
Holdings: Files of local families,especially the Robinson family.

LITCHFIELD (1729)
255 Charles Bancroft Hwy., Hudson 03051, Telephone 424-4055.
Previous names: Brenton's Farm, Naticook.

Litchfield Public Library, 269 Charles Bancroft Hwy., RFD 1, Hudson 03051,
Telephone 424-4044.
Hours: Mon. & Wed. 10-12 & 2-8, Tues.,Thurs., & Fri. 2-6, Sat. 11-1 (no
Sat. hours during July & Aug.).
Holdings: File of local newspaper HUDSON-LITCHFIELD NEWS and several defunct
local newspapers. Some town records.

LYNDEBOROUGH (1735)
P. O. Box 164, Lyndeborough 03082, Telephone 654-9653.
Previous names: Purgatory, Salem -Canada.

J. A. Tarbell Library, Box 54, Lyndeborough 03082, Telephone 654-6790.
Hours: Winter: Mon. 12-5 & 6-8, Wed. 9-4, Fri. 1-4. Summer: Mon. 9-3 &
6-8, Wed. 1-5, Fri. 1-4.
Holdings: Book collection. Clipping file.

Lyndeborough Historical Society, RR 1, Box 240, Lyndeborough 03082, no
telephone.
Hours: By appt.
Holdings: Vertical file.

*MANCHESTER (1751)
904 Elm St., Manchester 03101, Telephone 624-6455.
Previous names: Derryfield, Harrytown, Tyng's Town.

American-Canadian Genealogical Society, P. O. Box 668, Manchester 03105-
0668, Telephone 622-1554.
Hours: Wed. 1-9, Fri. 10-9, Sat. 9-4.
Holdings: Roman Catholic Church records from Quebec, Maine, Vermont,
New Hampshire and Massachusetts. Business records of local French-
Canadian undertaker. Records of the Association Cando-Amercaine. Files
on 5000 area families. Card file index for individual names. Quebec
map collection. Census records for Ossipee, Moultonborough and Concord.
Vital statistics file. Book collection on Acadia. Large book collection
on French-Canadian families. Files of over 30 French-Canadian genealogical publications including LIFELINE, ACADIA GENEALOGY EXCHANGE,
L'ACETERE and MEMOIRES DE LA SOCIETE GENEALOGIQUE CANADIENNE FRANCAISE.
Publications: AMERICAN-CANADIAN GENEALOGIST (quarterly journal available
at $3 per issue). Other publications include REPERTOIRES (marriage re-
ports) of New Hampshire Parishes including St. Joseph's of Manchester
($30), St. George's of Manchester ($22), St. Marie's of Manchester ($30),
and St. Paul's of Franklin ($18).

Association Cando-Amercaine, 52 Concord St., Manchester 03101, Telephone
625-8577.
Hours: Tues. through Thur. 9:30-2:30.
Holdings: Microfilm collection of French language newspapers from
Manchester, NH, Nashua, NH, Lowell, MA, and elsewhere in New England.
The files of late historian/folklorist Adelard Lambert. Scrapbook collection. Records of many local French-Canadian groups. Book collection
on French-Canadian families. Papers of many local families.
Publications: The organization is a non-profit fraternal insurance company but its quarterly magazine CANDO-AMERCAINE has articles of use to
genealogists.

Diocesan Museum, 435 Union St., Manchester 03104, Telephone 624-1729.
Hours: Tues, Thur., & Fri. 10-4, Sat. 10-12.
Holdings: Roman Catholic records for New Hampshire from 1848.

Geisel Library, St. Anselm's College, Manchester 03102-1310, Telephone
641-7300.
Hours: Mon. through Sat. 9-5.
Holdings: Small book collection of town history.

Manchester City Library, 405 Pine St., Manchester 03104-6199, Telephone
624-6550.
Hours: Winter: Mon., Tues., Thur. 9:30-9, Wed. 12:30-5:30, Fri. (;30-5:30,
Sat. 9-5. Summer: Mon. & Thur. 9:30-9, Tues. & Fri. 9:30-6, Wed. 10:30-6,
Sat. 9-5.
Holdings: Microfilm file of local daily UNION LEADER and N.H.SUNDAY NEWS.
Large book collection. 145 scrapbooks on microfilm and indexed.File of
telephone and city directory. File of HISTORICAL NEW HAMPSHIRE. Vertical
file.

with privately index and NEW HAMPSHIRE GENEALOGICAL RECORD.

Manchester Historic Association, 129 Amherst St., Manchester 03104, Telephone 622-7531.
Hours: Tues. through Fri. 9-4, Sat. 10-4.
Holdings: Large oral history tape collection. Records of many local companies including the Amoskeag Corporation. Papers of many families including Knox, Dunbar, Tilton, Green, Wheat, Newton and Elkins families. Manchester municipal records. School records. Town records from neighboring communities (Auburn, Bedford, Chester, Epping, Goffstown, Raymond and Londonderry). Records of two towns that became part of Manchester (Derryfield
and Amoskeag). Hillsborough and Rockingham county records. Special collections of Jewish and American Indian communities. Records of many groups
including DAR, JAR, Colonial Dames, Oddfellows, local churches and Rotary.
Large collection of diaries from Abbot, Stearns, Perkins, Tolman, Fisher,
Daniels, Griffin and Clark families. Files of over 30 defunct local newspapers including LA TRAVAILLEUR, AMOSKEAG REPRESETATIVE, DAILY MIRROR and
UNION DEMOCRAT. Militia records. High school yearbook collection. Map collection. Complete set of city and telephone directories. Clipping file.
Publications: REFLECTIONS (quarterly newsletter available with $25 annual
membership.

MASON (1749)
159 Fitchburg Rd., Mason 03048, Telephone 878-2070.
Previous names: No. #1.

Mason Historical Society, Mann House, Mason 03048, no telephone.
Hours: By appt.
Holdings: Cemetery records. School records. Some town records. Papers of
many local groups.

Mason Public Library, 16 Darling Hill Rd., Mason 03048, Telephone 878-3867.
Hours: Tues. 10-5, Wed. 1-4, Thur. 10-4 & 7-9, Sat. 10-1 (no Sat. hours in
summer).
Holdings: Local church records. Vertical file.

MERRIMACK (1746)
P. O. Box 27, Merrimack 03054, Telephone 424-3651.
Previous names: Lutwyhes Ferry, Naticook, Thornton's Ferry.

Merrimack Historical Society, P. O. Box 1525, Merrimack 03054, No telephone.
Hours: By appt.
Holdings: File on local families. Kittredge family papers. Records of the
McGaw Normal Institute, a defunct local school.

Merrimack Public Library, 470 Daniel Webster Hwy., Merrimack 03054, Tele-
phone 424-5021.
Hours: Mon. through Thur. 9-9, Fri. & Sat. 9-5 (July/Aug. Sat. hours 9-1).
Holdings: Small book collection. Some files on local groups.

MILFORD (1746)
1 Union Sq., Milford 03055, Telephone 673-3403.
Previous names: Duxbury School Farms, Mile Slip, Mill Ford, Monson, The
Falls.

Wadleigh Memorial Library, 21 Nashua St., Milford 03055, Telephone 673-2408.
Hours: Mon. through Wed. 9:30-8:30, Thur. through Sat. 9:30-5 (no Sat. in
July/Aug.)
Holdings: The Worcester Collection of local town history. Town records.
microfilm file of local newspaper MILFORD CABINET and several defunct loc-
al newspapers. Hutchinson family papers.

MONT VERNON (1803)
P. O. Box 4, Mont Vernon 03057, Telephone 673-9126.

Mont Vernon Historical Society, P. O. Box 15, Mont Vernon 03057, no tele-
phone.
Hours: Last Sat. & Sun. of each month 10-2 and by appt.
Holdings: Lamson family papers. Reconds of defunct school McCollom Inst.

*NASHUA (1746)
City Hall, Nashua 03061, Telephone 594-3305.
Previous names: Dunstable, Nashville.

Chandler Memorial Library and Ethnic Center, 257 Main St., Nashua 03060,
Telephone 594-3415.
Hours: Mon. through Wed., Fri. & Sat. 10-3 (closed Sat. May/Aug.),Thur.10-9
Holdings: Papers and records of many local ethnic associations.

Nashua Historical Society, 5 Abbott St., Nashua 03060, Telephone 883-0015.
Hours: By appt.
Holdings: Papers of many families especially the Spaulding, Speare, Lund and
Carter families. Cemetery lists. Some municipal records. Papers of many
local groups. File of city directories.Several files of local newspapers.
Large book collection.
Publications: newsletter (8 times per year for $10 annual membership).

Nashua Public Library, 2 Court St., Nashua 03060, Telephone 594-3412.
Hours: Mon. through Fri. 8:30-9, Sat. 8:30-5:30 (no hours July/Aug.), Sun.
1-5 (no hours May/Aug.).
Holdings: Large book collection including complete set WPA publications on
Nashua. Municipal records. Complete set of city directories. Complete
set of high school yearbooks. Microfilm file of local daily NASHUA TELE-
GRAPH and several defunct newspapers (NASHUA GAZETTE, NASHUA DAILY PRESS,
L'IMPARTIAL). Map and atlas collection. Vertical file. Large book collec=
tion of local churches. File of GRANITE STATE MONTHLY AND HISTORICAL NEW
HAMPSHIRE.

NEW BOSTON (1763)
282 Meadow Rd., New Boston 03070, Telephone 487-5571.
Previous names: Lanes Town.

New Boston Historical Society, 127 Butterfield Mill Rd., New Boston 03070,
no telephone.
Hours: By appt.
Holdings: Vertical file. Oral history tape collection. Records of Valley
View Farm.

Whipple Free Library, Main St., New Boston 03070, Telephone 487-3391.
Hours: Mon. & Wed. 10-8, Fri. 10-5, Sat. 9:30-12:30.
Holdings: File on local families.

NEW IPSWICH (1735)
Appleton Business Center, New Ipswich 03071, Telephone 878-3567.
Previous names: Ipswich.

New Ipswich Historical Society, P. O. Box 7, New Ipswich 03071, no telephone
Hours: By appt.
Holdings: Scrapbook collection. Records of defunct school Appleton Academy.

PELHAM (1746)
Town Hall, 6 Main St., Pelham 03076, Telephone 635-2040.

Pelham Public Library, 5 Main St., Pelham 03076, Telephone 635-7581.
Hours: Mon. & Thur. 10-8, Tues.,Wed. & Fri. 10-5.
Holdings: Some town records. Small book collection.

PETERBOROUGH (1760)
1 Grove St., Peterborough 03458, Telephone 924-6633.

Previous names: Souhegan.

Peterborough Historical Society, P. O. Box 58, 19 Grove St., Peterborough 03458, Telephone 924-3235.
Hours: Mon. through Fri. 10-4.
Holdings: Papers of several families especially the Steele, Morrison and Smith family. Cemetery records. Tow tax records. Business records of several local cotton mills. Vertical file. File of two local newspapers PETERBOROUGH TRANSCRIPT and MONADNOCK PERSPECTIVE.
Publications: newsletter (quarterly available for $5 annual dues).

Peterborough Town Library, Main & Concord Sts., Peterborough 03458, Telephone 924-6401.
Hours: Mon., Wed., Fri. 10-6, Tues. & Thur. 10-8, Sat. 9-1, Sun. 12-2 (no Sunday hours in summer).
Holdings: Large book collection. Many local newspapers on microfilm dating from 1833. :The papers of the McDowell Colony.

SHARON (1738)
3 Sliptown Rd., Sharon 03458, Telephone 924-7965.
Previous names: Peterborough Slip, Sliptown.

TEMPLE (1750)
P. O. Box 69, Temple 03084, Telephone 878-3873.
Previous names: Peterborough Slip, Sliptown.

Historical Society of Temple-see Mansfield Public Library.

Mansfield Public Library, P. O. Box 210, Temple 03084, Telephone 878-3100.
Hours: Mon. & Fri. 1:30-5, Tues. 10-12 & 1-5:30, Wed. 1:30-5 & 7-9, Sat. 2-4.
Holdings: Files on local families. Small book collection, includes holdings of the Historical Society of Temple.

WEARE (1735)
P. O. Box 90, Weáre 03281, Telephone 529-7575.
Previous names: Beverly-Canada, Halestown, Robiestown, Wearestown.

Weare Historical Society, P. O. Box 33, Weare 03281, no telephone.
Hours: By appt.
Holdings: Cemetery lists. File on local families.

Weare Public Library, 9 East Rd., P. O. Box 115, Weare 03281, Telephone 529-2044.
Hours: Mon. & Thur. 10-8, Wed. 10-6, Sat. 10-12 (no Sat. hours in summer).
Holdings: Small book collection.

WILTON (1749)
P. O. Box 83, Wilton 03086, Telephone 654-9451.
Previous names: No. #2.

Wilton Historical Society-see Wilton Public & Gregg Free Library.

Wilton Public & Gregg Free Library, Forest St., Box 240, Wilton 03086, Telephone 654-2581.
Hours: Mon., Wed., Fri 2-5, Tues. & Thur. 9-12 & 2-8, Sat. 9-12.
Holdings: Large book collection. Cemetary records. Some newspaper files, includes holdings of Wilton Historical Society.

WINDSOR (1798)
HC 68, Box 378, Hillsborough 03244, Telephone 478-3293.
Previous names: Campbell's Gore, Wheeler's Gore.

MERRIMACK COUNTY

Registrar of Deeds
163 North Main St.
Concord 03301
Telephone 228-0101

Registrar of Probate
163 North Main St.
Concord 03301
Telephone 224-9589

ALLENSTOWN (1721)
P. O. Box 231, Suncook 03275, Telephone 485-3111.

ANDOVER (1779)
P. O. Box 61, Andover 03216, Telephone 735-5332.
Previous names: Brown's Town, Emerystown, New Breton.

Andover Historical Society, Box 62, Potter Place 03216, Telephone 735-5721.
Hours: By appt.
Holdings: Town records. Records of Kearsarge Grange. Business records, especially from Andover Workshop and Home Industries.

Andover Public Library, RFD 1, Box 2445, Andover 03216, Telephone 735-5752.
Hours: Mon. 6:30-8:30, Wed. 9-12 & 6:30-8:30, Thur. 12:30-4:30.
Holdings: Small book collection.

William Adams Bachelder Library, P. O. Box 128, East Andover 03216, Telephone 735-5333.
Hours: Tues. 1:30-5 & 6:30-8:30, Thur. 6:30-8:30, Fri. 1:30-5.
Holdings: Small book collection.

BOSCAWEN (1732)
17 High St., Boscawen 03303, Telephone 796-2426.
Previous names: Contoocook.

Boscawen Branch Library, Boscawan 03303, no telephone.
Hours: Mon. 3-6:30, Wed. 3-7.
Holdings: Small book collection.

Boscawen Historical Society, Box 3067, Boscawen 03303, no telephone.
Hours: By appt.
Holdings: Small collection of local family diaries.

Boscawen Public Library, P. O. Box 3242, Boscawen 03303, Telephone 796-2442.
Hours: Tues. 2:30-6, Thur. 3-7.
Holdings: Town records. Merrimack County Nursing Home records. Merrimack County Farm records. Small book collection.

BOW (1727)
10 Grandview Rd., Bow 03304, Telephone 225-2683.
Previous names: Pembroke.

BRADFORD (1787)
P. O. Box 607, Bradford 03221, Telephone 938-2288.
Previous names: Bradfordton, New Bradford.

Bradford Historical Society, P. O. Box 551, Bradford 03221, no telephone.
Hours: By appt.
Holdings: Files on local families including the Presby, Cressy, Sweet, Sweat Hoyt, Frank, Ward and Clough families. Files on ownership of local property Scattered files of local newspapers including the (Bradford) VISITOR. Some town records.

CANTERBURY (1727)

P. O. Box 500, Canterbury 03224, Telephone 783-9955.

Canterbury Historical Society-see Elkins Library.

Canterbury-Shaker Village, 288 Shaker Rd., Canterbury 03224, Telephone 783-9511.
Hours: Fri. & Sat. 10-5, Sun. 12-5.
Holdings: Archives and papers of all 19 Shaker Societies in America.

Elkins Library, 7 Center St., Canterbury 03224-2401, Telephone 783-4386.
Hours: Mon. & Thur. 2-8, Wed. 9-5, first & third Sat. of each month 9-11.
Holdings: Cemetery lists. Files on local families. Verticle file. Includes holdings of Canterbury Historical Society.

CHICHESTER (1727)
Town Hall, Main St., Chichester 03263, Telephone 798-5808.

Chichester Historical Society, 26 Mulberry St., Chichester 03743, no telephone.
Hours: Sun. mid-June - Sept. 1-4,& by appt.
Holdings: Cemetery lists.

Chichester Town Library, P. O. Box 582, Main St., Chichester 03263, Telephone 798-5613.
Hours: Mon. & Tues, Thur. 6-8, Wed. 2-4, Sat. 11-3.
Holdings: Some town records.

*CONCORD (1725)
41 Green St., Concord 03301, Telephone 225-8500.
Previous names: Penacook, Romford, Rumford.

Concord Public Library, 45 Green St., Concord 03301, Telephone 225-8670.
Hours: Mon. through Thur. 9-9, Fri. & Sat. 9-5, Sun. 1-5. Summer: Mon. & Tues. 9-8:30, Wed. through Fri. 9-5:30, Sat. 9-2.
Holdings: Files on many local families especially the Abbots, Bean and McLane family. Files of many local defunct newspapers and the current daily CONCORD MONITOR. Papers of many local social groups and churches. Business records including several local insurance companies. Large book collection. Municipal records. School records. Cemetery lists. Voting lists. Holdings of Heritage Concord Inc. (file on 700 Concord buildings and homes including record of ownership). Many of the library holdings were microfilmed with the original sent to the New Hampshire Historical Society and the library retaining the microfilms.

Heritage Concord Inc., - see Concord Public Library.

New Hampshire Historical Society, 30 Park St., Concord 03301, Telephone 225-3381.
Hours: Mon. through Fri. 9-4, Sat. 12-4.
Holdings: 4000 genealogies (approximately one third unpublished). 3000 files of local government records. 4000 files of local churches and religious groups. Large cemetery records collection. Revolutionary War pension records. Complete runs of city and state directories. Large map collection. Small collection of local historical society publications. File of five current state genealogical publications (FAMILY TRACES, KINSHIP KRONICLE, GENEALOGICAL RECORD OF STRAFFORD COUNTY, NEW HAMPSHIRE GENEALOGICAL RECORD and NEWSLETTER of the New Hampshire Society of Genealogists). Files of 679 pre-1900 newspapers from 108 communities. 800 family diaries. 8000 individual collections of family papers including Abbot, McLane, Wadleigh, Walker, Tuttle, Wallace, Ward, Webster, Watson, Whitcomb, Towle, Thompson, Thornton, Swett, Baldwin, Blood, Campbell and Dow families. Includes holdings of the New Hampshire Society of Genealogists.
Publications: newsletter and HISTORICAL NEW HAMPSHIRE (quarterlys that come $30 annual dues. Current book titles INDEX TO GENEALOGIES IN NEW HAMPSHIRE

TOWN HISTORIES by William Copeley ($6).

New Hampshire Society of Genealogists-see New Hampshire Historical Society.

New Hampshire State Archives, 71 Fruit St., Concord 03301, Telephone 271-2236.
Hours: Mon. through Fri. 8-4.
Holdings: Most state and numerous colonial era government records and documents. Many pre-1810 town records. Census record for 1732, 1741, 1760, 1800, 1850, 1860, 1870 and 1880.

New Hampshire State Bureau of Vital Records, 6 Hazen Dr., Concord 03301, Telephone 271-4650.
Hours: Mon. through Fri. 8:15-4.
Holdings: All state records of deaths, marriages and divorces before 1938 and births before 1901 are available to the general public. Volunteers from the New Hampshire Society of Genealogists are available to assist the public.

New Hampshire State Division of Historic Preservation, Fruit Ave., Concord 03301, Telephone 271-3558.
Hours: Mon. through Fri. 8-4.
Holdings: File on all homes and other structures nominated to be in the Historic American Buildings Survey or the National Register of Historic Sites.

New Hampshire State Library, 20 Park St., Concord 03301, Telephone 271-2394.
Hours: Mon. through Fri. 8-4:30.
Holdings: 100 regimental histories. Several hundred biographies. 100 genealogies. 300 town histories. Files of New Hampshire publications include several hundred newspaper titles. Clipping files on most New Hampshire towns. Files of 100 state families. State muster records. Census records.

St. Paul School, 325 Pleasant St., Concord 03301, Telephone 225-3341.
Hours: Mon. through Fri. 9-5.
Holdings: Family papers of several former head masters.

                          DANBURY (1795)
Box 86A, Ragged Mountain Rd., Danbury 03230, Telephone 768-3313.

George Gamble Library, Rt. 104, Danbury 03230, no telephone.
Hours: Sat. 12-4.
Holdings: Some town records. Small book collection.

                          DUNBARTON (1735)
1011 School St., Dunbarton 03045, Telephone 774-3547.
Previous names: Gorham's-town, Starkstown, Stark Town.

                          EPSOM (1727)
P. O. Box 10, Epsom 03234, Telephone 736-4825.

Epsom Historical Society,-see Epsom Public Library.

Epsom Public Library, Dover Rd., Epsom 03234, Telephone 736-9920.
Hours: Mon. 10-1, Wed. 10-7, Thur. 10-5, Sat. 10-3 (10-12 in summer).
Holdings: File on local families especially the Bickford family. Cemetery records. Town records. Small book collection includes holdings of Epsom Historical Society.

                          *FRANKLIN (1828)
P. O. Box 235, Franklin 03235, Telephone 934-3109.
Previous names: Pemigewasset Village, Salisbury Lower Village.

Franklin Historical Society, P. O. Box 43, Franklin 03235, no telephone.

Hours: By appt.
Holdings: Notes and papers of late local historian Alice Shepard. Clipping file. Scrapbook collection. Several files of local defunct newspapers.

Franklin Public Library, 310 Central St., Franklin 03235, Telephone 934-2911.
Hours: Mon., Wed., Fri. 9-8, Tues. & Thur. 9-5 (no Sat. hours in summer).
Holdings: Small book collection. Some municipal records. Vertical file. Several files of defunct local newspapers including MERRIMACK JOURNAL. Collection of city directories. Papers of Aiken and Webster families.

HENNIKER (1768)
2 Depot Hill Rd., Henniker 03242, Telephone 428-3240.
Previous names: New Marlborough, No. #6, Todd's Town.

Henniker Historical Society,-see Tucker Free Library.

Tucker Free Library, Box 688, Western Ave., Henniker 03242, Telephone 428-3471.
Hours: Mon. 10-7, Tues. & Fri. 10-5, Wed. 10-5 & 7-9, Sat. 9-1 (no Sat. hours in July and Aug.)
Holdings: Some town records. Small book collection. Holdings of Henniker Historical Society (Brown, Swett, & Patterson family papers. File of THE DEAF MUTE'S FRIEND).

HILL (1753)
P. O. Box 251, Hill 03243, Telephone 934-3055.
Previous names: New Chester.

Hill Historical Society, Hill 03243, no telephone.
Hours: By appt.
Holdings: Files of local families. Cemetery lists. Early town and school records.
Publications: newsletter (quarterly $5 annual membership).

Hill Public Library, Hill 03243, no telephone.
Hours: Tues. 1:30-4:30 & 7-8:30, Wed. 1-4.
Holdings: Small book collection.

HOOKSETT (1822)
16 Main St., Hooksett 03106, Telephone 485-9534.
Previous names: Chester Woods, Hanna-Ko-Kees-Hills, Rowe's Corner, White Pine Country.

Hooksett Historical Society, 68 Whitehall Rd., Hooksett 03106, no telephone
Hours: By appt.
Holdings: Town records. School records.

HOPKINTON (1735)
P. O. Box 169, Contoocook 03229, Telephone 746-3180.
Previous names:Line of Towns #5, New Hopkinton.

New Hampshire Antiquarian Society, RR 5, Box 251, Contoocook 03229, no telephone.
Hours: By appt.
Holdings: Large file on local genealogy including many unpublished manuscripts. 200 diaries of the Patch family.

LOUDON (1773)
P. O. Box 7837, Loudon 03301, Telephone 798-4542.

Loudon Historical Society, Old Fire Station, Loudon 03301, no telephone.
Hours: By appt.
Holdings: Town records. Cemetary records. Oral history tape collection.

NEWBURY (1754)
P. O. Box 253, Newbury 03255, Telephone 763-5326.
Previous names: Dantzic, Fishersfield, Hereford.

Newbury Historical Society, P. O. Box 176, Newbury 03255, no telephone.
Hours: By appt.
Holdings: Town records. Vertical file. Papers of late local historian
Ernest Sherman. Cemetery records. Index card file on vital statistics.
Mixed files of area newspapers.

Newbury Public Library, Box 245, Rt. 103, Newbury 03255, Telephone 763-
5803.
Hours: Mon. 2-8, Tues. 10-1, Wed. 2-5, Sat. 10-12.
Holdings: Small book collection.

NEW LONDON (1753)
P. O. Box 314, New London 03257, Telephone 526-4046.
Previous names: Alexandria Addition, Heidelberg, New Londonderry.

Susan Colgate Cleveland Library, Colby-Sawyer College, Main St., New London
03257, Telephone 526-2010.
Hours: Mon. through Thur. 8-11, Fri. 8-5, Sat. 12-5, Sun. 12-11.
Holdings: Cleveland family papers.

Tracy Memorial Library, Main St., P. O. Box 1919, New London 03257, Telephone 526- 4656.
Hours: Winter: Tues. 9-8, Wed. 9-5, Thur. 1-8, Sat. 9:30-12. Summer: Tues.
9:30-8, Wed. & Fri. 9:30-5, Thur. 1-8, Sat. 9:30-12.
Holdings: Some town records.

NORTHFIELD (1780)
21 Summer St., Northfield 03276, Telephone 286-4482.
Previous names: Factory Village, North Hill.

PEMBROKE (1728)
311 Pembroke St., Pembroke 03275, Telephone 485-4747.
Previous names: Buckstreet, Lovell's Town, Lovewell's Town, Suncook.

Pembroke Historical Society, 246 Pembroke St., Pembroke 03275, no telephone
Hours: By appt.
Holdings: Town records. School records. Small collection of published and
unpublished genealogies.

PITTSFIELD (1782)
P. O. Box 98, Pittsfield 03263., Telephone 435-6773.

Carpenter Memorial Library, 31 Main St., Pittsfield 03263, Telephone 435-
8406.
Hours: Mon. & Thur. 2-8, Tues. & Wed. 2-5, Fri. 10-5, Sat. 10-12. No Sat.
hours in summer.
Holdings: Small book collection. Files on local families. Town records.
Clipping file.

SALISBURY (1736)
Box 180, Salisbury 03268, Telephone 648-2473.
Previous names: Baker's Town, Gerrishtown, New Salisbury, Stevenstown.

Salisbury Free Library, Box 100, Salisbury 03268, Telephone 648-2278.
Hours: Tues. 1-5, Thur. 9-12, Fri. 6-8, Sat. 1-4.
Holdings: Small book collection. Some town records.

Salisbury Historical Society, Box 102, West Salisbury Rd., Salisbury 03268.
no telephone.
Hours: By appt.

Holdings: Records of Old Baptist Meeting House. Some town records.

SUTTON (1748)
P. O. Box 443, Sutton 03273, Telephone 927-4416.
Previous names: Perrystown.

Muster Field Farm Museum-Harvey Homestead, P. O. Box 120, No. Sutton, no telephone.
Hours: By appt.
Holdings: Harvey family papers.

Old Store Museum of South Sutton, South Sutton 03273, no telephone.
Hours: By appt.
Holdings: Collection of unpublished manuscripts on local history.

Sutton Historical Society, P. O. Box 462, South Sutton 03273, no telephone.
Hours: By appt.
Holdings: Computerized genealogical data sheets on local families going back to 1784. Church records. Town records. Business records. Oral history tape collection. Index of names in town records.
Publications: SUTTON NOW AND THEN (quarterly newsletter, $5 annual dues).

WARNER (1735)
RFD 2, Box 373, Warner 03278, Telephone 456-3362.
Previous names: Kearsarge Gore, Jennesstown, Line of Town #1, New Amesbury, No. #1, Robies Town, Ryetown, Waterloo.

Pillsbury Free Library, P. O. Box 278, Warner 03278, Telephone 465-2656.
Hours: Tues. 9-12 & 2-5, Wed. 2-5, Thur. 9-12 & 2-8, Sat. 9-12.
Holdings: Small collection of genealogies. Clipping files.

Warner Historical Society, P. O. Box 189, Warner 03278, Telephone 456-2437.
Hours: By appt.
Holdings: George, Cogswell and Wilkins family papers. Collection of 200 oral history tapes. Scrapbook collection.
Publications: Newsletter (quarterly $5 annual dues).

WEBSTER (1860)
RFD 7, Box 391, Penacook 03303, Telephone 648-2723.

Webster Free Public Library, Rt. 5, Box 325, Webster 03303, Telephone 648-2076.
Hours: Mon. 9-2 & 6-8, Wed. 9-8.
Holdings: Small book collection. Some town records. File of local newspaper WEBSTER GRAPEVINE.

Webster Old Meeting House Society, Rt. 5, Box 256, Webster 03303, no telephone.
Hours: By appt.
Holdings: Town records. Small collection of diaries. Some records of local groups.

WILMOT (1807)
Box 65, Wilmot 03287, Telephone 526-4802.

Wilmot Historical Society, P. O. Box 83, Wilmot 03287, no telephone.
Hours: By appt.
Holdings: Town records.

Wilmot Public Library, North Wilmot Rd., Wilmot 03287, Telephone 526-6804.
Hours: Mon. 6:30-8:30, Tues. 3-5 (no Tues. hours in winter), Wed. 10-4 & 6:30-8:30, Thur. 3-5, Sat. 10-12.
Holdings: Small book collection. Some town records. Clipping file.

Wilmot Town History Committee, Town Hall, Wilmot 03287, no telephone.
Hours: By appt.
Holdings: Several hundred questionaires on family origins and history.

ROCKINGHAM COUNTY

Registrar of Deeds
Administration and Justice Bldg.
1 Hampton Rd.
Exeter 03833
Telephone 772-4712

Registrar of Probate
County Office Bldg.
Exeter 03833
Telephone 772-9347

ATKINSON (1767)
Town Hall, 21 Academy Ave., Atkinson 03811, Telephone 362-4920.

Atkinson Historical Society, 10 Academy Ave., Atkinson 03811, no telephone.
Hours: By appt.
Holdings: Town records. Collection of local genealogies. Records of
Atkinson Grange. Records of defunct local school Atkinson Academy.

AUBURN (1845)
P. O. Box 309, Auburn 03032, Telephone 483-2281.
Previous names: Chester Woods, Chester West Parish, Long Meadow.

Auburn Historical Society-see Griffin Public Library.

Griffin Public Library, P. O. Box 308, Auburn 03032, Telephone 483-5374.
Hours: Tues. 6:30-8, Fri. 3-5, Sat. 10-1 (summer only).
Holdings: Small book collection. Small collection of local diaries. In-
cludes holdings of Auburn Historical Society.

BRENTWOOD (1741)
RFD 1, Dalton Rd., Brentwood 03883, Telephone 642-8817.
Previous names: Brentwood Parish, Brintwood Parish, Keeneborough.

Mary E. Bartlett Memorial Library, RFD 1, Dalton Rd., Brentwood 03833, Telephone 642-3355.
Hours: Winter: Mon. 5-8, Tues. & Wed. 12:30-5:30, Thur. 3-8, Fri. 9-12, Sat.
9-1. Summer: Mon. & Thur. 5-8, Tues. & Wed. 1-5, Sat. 9-1.
Holdings: Town records. Small book collection.

CANDIA (1763)
74 High St., Candia 03034, Telephone 483-5573.
Previous names: Charmingfare.

Fitz Museum, P. O. Box 347, Candia 03034, no telephone.
Hours: By appt.
Holdings: Fitz family papers. Lane family papers. Cemetery records.

Smyth Public Library, P. O. Box 256, 194 High St., Candia 03034, Telephone
483-8245.
Hours: Tues. & Wed. 1-9, Thurs. 1-6, Fri. 9-12 & 5-8, Sat. 9-4 (9-12 July-
Aug.).
Holdings: Some town records. Small book collection.

CHESTER (1722)
P. O. Box 275, Chester 03036, Telephone 887-3636.
Previous names: Cheshire.

Chester Historical Society, Town Hall, Chester 03036, no telephone.
Hours: By appt.
Holdings: Files on local families, especially the Bell and Boughton families. Vertical file. Town records. Small book collection.

Chester Public Library, 3 Chester St., Chester 03036, Telephone 887-3404.
Hours: Mon. & Wed. 6-9, Tues. & Thur. 10-8, Fri. 10-5.
Holdings: Small book collection.

DANVILLE (1760)
72 Beach Plain Rd., Danville 03819, Telephone 382-8253.
Previous names: Hawke.

Colby Memorial Library, P. O. Box 10, Danville 03819, Telephone 382-6733.
Hours: Winter: Mon., Tues., Thur. 2:30-7:30, Wed. 9-12, Sat. 9-12 (during school year). Summer: Tues. & Thur. 3-8, Wed. 9-12.
Holdings: Small book collection. Town records. Papers of the Colby family. Collection of local diaries. Local probate records. Includes holdings of the Hawke Historical Society of Danville.

Hawke Historical Society of Danville-see Colby Memorial Library.

DEERFIELD (1766)
P. O. Box 159, Deerfield 03037, Telephone 463-8811.
Previous names: Nottingham.

Deerfield Historical Society, Town Hall, 167 South Rd., Deerfield 03037, no telephone.
Hours: By appt.
Holdings: Files on local families especially the Mallon family. Collection of local deeds. Lists of local burial plots. Records of local Baptist and Congregational churches. Files of defunct local newspapers.

Philbrick-James Library, 4 Old Center Rd., Deerfield 03037, Telephone 463-7187.
Hours: Mon. & Wed. 6:30-8:30, Tues. 9-12, Thur. 1-5, Sat. 10-3.
Holdings: Small book collection.

DERRY (1827)
48 East Broadway, Derry 03038, Telephone 432-6105.

Derry Historical Society, 65 Birch St., Derry 03038, no telephone.
Hours: Sun. 2-4 and by appt.
Holdings: Small book collection. Some papers of the Montgomery family. Cemetery lists. Scattered files of defunct local newspapers. Scrapbook collection.

Derry Public Library: 64 E. Broadway, Derry 03038, Telephone 432-6140.
Hours: Mon. through Thur. 10-8, Fri. 10-5, Sat. 9-5 (no Sat. hours in summer).
Holdings: Large book collection. Microfilm file of local newspaper DERRY NEWS.

Taylor Library, P. O. Box 110, 49 E. Derry Rd., E. Derry 03041, Telephone 432-7186.
Hours: Mon. & Wed. 10-5, Tues. & Thur. 12-8,
Holdings: Adams family diaries. Records of many local groups. School records. Tax records. Records of Adam Female Academy. Records of First Parish Church of E. Derry. Map collection. Small book collection.

EAST KINGSTON (1738)
24 Depot Rd., East Kingston 03827, Telephone 642-8794.
Previous names: Kingston East Parish.

East Kingston Public Library, 41 Dept Rd., East Kingston 03827, Telephone
642-8333.
Hours: Mon. 9-12, 1-5 & 6-8, Wed. 1-5 & 6-8, Fri. 9-12, Sat. 9-1 (no Sat.
hours in summer).
Holdings: Town records, Vertical file. Card file on local individuals
and their land holdings.

EPPING (1741)
157 Main St., Epping 03042, Telephone 679-8288.

Epping Historical Society, P. O. Box 348, Epping 03042, no telephone.
Hours: By appt.
Holdings: Computerized list of vital statistics. File on local families.

Harvey-Mitchell Memorial Library, P. O. Box 355, 52 Main St., Epping 03042,
Telephone 679-5944.
Hours: Mon. & Tues. 1-5, Wed. & Thur. 1-5 & 7-9, Fri. 10-12 & 1-5.
Holdings: Some town records.

EXETER (1638)
10 Front St., Exeter 03833, Telephone 778-0591.
Previous names: Squamscott, Squamscott Falls.

American Independence Museum, 1 Governor's Lane, Exeter 03833, Telephone
772-2622.
Hours: Nov. 1st to April 30th Tues. & Sat. 12-3. May 1st to Oct. 31st Tues
through Sat. 10-4, Sun. 12-4.
Holdings: Papers of the Ladd, Gilman, Folsom, Chadwick and Terry families.

Archival Records, Phillips Exeter Academy, Exeter 03833, Telephone 772-4311
ext. 326.
Hours: Mon. through Fri. 9-4 and by appt.
Holdings: Families papers of founders, faculty and alumni.

Exeter Historical Society, 47 Front St., Exeter 03833, Telephone 778-2335.
Hours: Tues., Thur., & Sat. 2-5.
Holdings: File of many family papers especially the Folsom, Bean, Gilman,
and Robin families. Map collection. Files of local defunct newspapers.
Publications: newsletter (semi-annual $20. annual membership).

Exeter Public Library, Founder's Park, Exeter 03833, Telephone 772-3101.
Hours. Mon. through Thur. 10-8, Fri. & Sat. 10-5 (no Sat. hours in summer).
Holdings: 1000 books on local family and town history. File on local fam-
ilies. File of local newspaper EXETER NEWS-LETTER. File of KINSHIP
KRONICLE. Records of the New England Antiquities Research Association.
Includes holdings of the Rockingham Society of Genealogists.

Rockingham Society of Genealogists-see Exeter Public Library.

FREMONT (1764)
168 Scribner Rd. Fremont 03044, Telephone 895-2226.
Previous names: Poplin.

Fremont Historical Society, Main St., Fremont 03044, no telephone.
Hours: By appt.
Holdings: Small book collection. Map collection. Beede family papers.

Fremont Public Library, Beede Rd., Fremont 03044, Telephone 895-9543.
Hours: Tues. & Thur. 4-8, Sat. 9-1.
Holdings: Some town records.

New England Historical Research Associates, 225 South Rd., Fremont 03044,
no telephone.
Hours: By appt.

Holdings: 2500 volume collection of town and family histories. Lists of individual book titles located at area libraries. Correspondence file on family history. This is a professional genealogical research firm.

GREENLAND (1704)
575 Portsmouth Ave., Greenland 03840, Telephone 431-7111.

Greenland Historical Society, 459 Portsmouth Ave., Greenland 03840, no telephone.
Hours: By appt.
Holdings: Records of local Methodist and community churches.

Weeks Public Library, Post Rd., P. O. Box 430, Greenland 03840, Telephone 436-8548.
Hours: Mon., Wed., Fri. 10-8, Sat. 10-2.
Holdings: Small book collection. Some town records. Vertical file.

HAMPSTEAD (1749)
11 Main St., Hampstead 03841, Telephone 329-6840.
Previous names: Timberlane Parish, Timberland.

Hampstead Public Library, P. O. Box 109, Main St., Hampstead 03841, Telephone 329-6411.
Hours: Mon. & Wed. 1-6, Tues. & Thur. 9-9 (summer hours are 9-8), Sat. 9-1.
Holdings: Vertical file. File on local families. Some town records.

HAMPTON (1639)
136 Winnacunnet Rd., Hampton 03842, Telephone 926-0406.
Previous names: Winnecunnet.

Hampton Historical Society, Tuck Memorial Museum, 40 Park Ave., Hampton 03842, Telephone 926-3287.
Hours: July-Aug. 1-4 daily and by appt.
Holdings: Large book collection. Large scrapbook collection.
Publications: GATHERINGS FROM THE GREEN (quarterly $10 annual membership).

Lane Memorial Library, Academy Ave., Hampton 03842, Telephone 926-3368.
Hours: Mon. through Thur. 9-8, Fri. & Sat. 9-5.
Holdings: Small book collection. Some town records. File of local newspaper HAMPTON UNION. Vertical file.

HAMPTON FALLS (1723)
Town Office, 1 Drinkwater Rd., Hampton Falls 03844, Telephone 926-4618.
Previous names: Third Parish.

Hampton Falls Free Public Library, 45 Exeter Rd., Hampton Falls 03844-2004, Telephone 926-3682.
Hours: Mon. 10-12 & 1-5, Tues. 1-5 & 6-8, Wed. & Sat. 9-12, Thur. 1-5.
Holdings: Small book collection.

Hampton Falls Historical Society, Box 104, Hampton Falls 03844, no telephone.
Hours: By appt.
Holdings: Cemetery lists. Some town records.

KENSINGTON (1737)
95 Amesbury Rd., Kensington 03833, Telephone 772-5423.

Kensignton Historical Society-see Kensington Social and Public Library.

Kensington Social and Public Library, 126 Amesbury Rd., Kensington 03827, Telephone 772-5022.
Hours: Tues. 1-5 & 6-8, Wed. & Fri. 1-5, Thur. 1-6 & 6-8, Sat. 10-1.

Holdings: Book collection. Obituary file. Scrapbook collection. File on many local families including Page, Brown, Black, Gove, Henry, Prescott, Sanborn, Cram, Dearborn, and Shaw families. School records. Town records. Collection of family bibles. Business records. Farm ledgers. Includes holdings of Kensington Historical Society.

KINGSTON (1694)
P. O. Box 657, Kingston 03848, Telephone 642-3112.
Previous names: King's Town.

Kingston Improvement and Historical Society-see Nichols Memorial Library.

Nichols Memorial Library, 169 Main St., P. O. Box 128, Kingston 03848, Telephone 642-3521.
Hours: Winter: Tues. through Thur. 10-8, Fri. & Sat. 10-3. Summer: Tues. & Wed. 10-7, Thur. & Fri. 10-3.
Holdings: Small book collection. Papers and notes of George Herman, a late local historian. Includes holdings of Kingston Improvement and Historical Society.

LONDONDERRY (1722)
268 Mammoth Rd., Londonderry 03053, Telephone 432-1133.
Previous names: Nutfield.

Leach Library, 276 Mammoth Rd., Londonderry 03053-3004, Telephone 432-1132.
Hours: Mon. & Wed. 9-6, Tues. & Thur. 10-8, Fri. 9-5, Sat. 10-4 (no summer hours).
Holdings: Some town records. Cemetery lists. Small book collection. Includes holdings of the Londonderry Historical Society.

Londonderry Historical Society-see Leach Library.

NEW CASTLE (1693)
P. O. Box 367, New Castle 03854, Telephone 431-6710.
Previous names: Fort William & Mary, Great Island.

New Castle Archives and Records Committee, New Castle 03854, Telephone 431-6854.
Hours: By appt.
Holdings: All town records. Pre-1900 Rockingham County probate, trust and property records.

New Castle Historical Society-see New Castle Public Library.

New Castle Public Library, P. O. Box 329, Westworth Rd., New Castle 03854, Telephone 431-6773.
Hours: Mon. 1-7, Wed. & Thur. 11-5.
Holdings: Index card file on pre-1900 vital statistics. Meloon family papers includes holding of New Castle Historical Society.

NEWFIELDS (1849)
P. O. Box 45, Newfields 03856, Telephone 772-3149.
Previous names: South Newmarket.

Newfields Public Library, P. O. Box 200, Newfields 03856, Telephone 778-8169.
Hours: Tues. 1-6, Fri. 1-4 & 6:30 - 8:30.
Holdings: Some town records.

NEWINGTON (1764)
Town Offices, 205 Nimble Hill Rd., Newington 03801, Telephone 436-7640.
Previous names: Bloody Point, Newington Parish.

Langdon Public Library, RT 151, Nimble Hill Rd., Newington 03801,

Telephone 436-5154.
Hours: Winter: Wed. 1-5:30, Thur. 1-6:30, Fri. 1-6, Sat. 11-6. Summer:
Wed. & Fri. 1-5, Thur. 1-6:30, Sat. 11-5.
Holdings: Files on local families especially the Frank, Hoyt, Furber and
Pickering families. Some town records. Vertical file. Includes the hold-
ings of the Newington Historical Society.

Newington Historical Society-see Langdon Public Library.

NEWMARKET (1737)
Town Hall, Main St., Newmarket 03857, Telephone 659-3617.

Newmarket Historical Society, Stone School Museum, Newmarket 03857, Telephone 659-3652.
Hours: By appt.
Holdings: Cemetery index. Records of many local church and community
groups. Records of the Newmarket Mfg. Co.

Newmarket Public Library, 1 Elm St., Newmarket 03857, Telephone 659-5311.
Hours: Mon. & Wed. 2-8, Tues., Thur., & Fri. 9-5, Sat. 9-1.
Holdings: Small book collection. Some town records. File of local news-
paper TRI-TOWN TRANSCRIPT.

NEWTON (1749)
P. O. Box 375, Newton 03858, Telephone 382-4096.
Previous names: New Town.

Gale Library, 16 South Main St., P. O. Box 208, Newton 03858, Telephone
382-4691.
Hours: Mon., Wed., Fri. 12-8, Tues & Sat. 10-1 (no Tues. & Sat. hours in
July, Aug.).
Holdings: Town records.

NORTH HAMPTON (1742)
P. O. Box 141, North Hampton 03862, Telephone 964-6029.
Previous names: North Hill, North Parish.

North Hampton Historical Society-see North Hampton Public Library.

North Hampton Public Library, 235 Atlantic Ave., P. O. Box 628, North
Hampton 03862, Telephone 964-6326.
Hours: Mon. & Wed. 10-8, Tues., Thur. & Fri. 10-5, Sat. 9-1.
Holdings: Small book collection. Town records on microfilm. Clipping
file. Small diary collection. Scrapbook collection. Index to cemeter-
ies. Includes holdings of North Hampton Historical Society.

NORTHWOOD (1773)
P. O. Box 314, Northwood 03261, Telephone 942-5422.
Previous names: Northwood Narrows, North Woods.

Chesley Memorial Library, P. O. Box 157, Northwood 03261, Telephone 942-
5472.
Hours: Mon. & Tues. 10-5, Wed. & Thur. 10-2 & 6-8, Sat. 10-2.
Holdings: Small book collection. Vertical file. Some town records.

Northwood Historical Society, Bryant Library, Northwood Narrows 03261,
no telephone.
Hours: By appt.
Holdings: Cemetary lists. Collection of unpublished manuscripts on local
history.

NOTTINGHAM (1722)
P. O. Box 114, Nottingham 03290, Telephone 679-5022.

Blaisdell Memorial Library, P. O. Box 115, Nottingham 03290, Telephone 679-8484.
Hours: Winter: Mon. & Wed. 10:30-8:30, Tues. & Fri. 9-4, Thur. 9-3:30, Sat. 9-1. Summer: Mon. & Wed. 6:30-8:30, Tues. & Thur. 9-5, Sat. 9-1.
Holdings: Town records on microfilm. Files on local families. Includes holdings of Nottingham Historical Society.

Nottingham Historical Society-see Blaisdell Memorial Library.

PLAISTOW (1742)
Town Hall, 145 Main St., Plaistow 03865, Telephone 382-8129.

Plaistow Public Library, P. O. Box 186, Plaistow 03865, Telephone 382-6011.
Hours: Mon. through Thur. 9-8:30, Fri. 9-5, Sat. 9-2.
Holdings: Town records. Regimental history collection. Book collection. File of local newspaper PLAISTOW-HAMPSTEAD NEWS.

*PORTSMOUTH (1653)
P. O. Box 628, Portsmouth 03802, Telephone 431-2000, ext. 207.
Previous names: Piscataqua, Strawberry Banke.

Moffatt-Ladd House, 154 Market St., Portsmouth 03801, Telephone 436-8221.
Hours: June 5th-Oct. 15th: Mon. through Sat. 10-4, Sun. 2-5 and by appt.
Holdings: Genealogical records of the Moffatt and Ladd families.

Portsmouth Athenaeum, P. O. Box 848, 9 Market Sq., Portsmouth 03801, Telephone 431-2538.
Hours: By appt.
Holdings: Large book collection. Records of many local groups including several insurance companies. Local police and fire department records. Large collection of local deeds. Papers of many families especially the Wendell, Woodbury, Pepperell, Frost, Sandford, Pierce and Langdon families. Files of many local publications including NEW HAMPSHIRE FREEMASON, NEW HAMPSHIRE GAZETTE, TRESTLE BOARD (a masonic publication), PORTSMOUTH HERALD and many defunct local newspapers. Customs records. Index of local graveyards. Records of North and St. John's Churches. Proper name index to the holdings. Files on local homes. Index for NEW HAMPSHIRE GAZETTE. Includes holdings of Portsmouth Historical Society.

Portsmouth Historical Society-see Portsmouth Athenaeum.

Portsmouth Public Library, 8 Islington St., Portsmouth 03801, Telephone 427-1540.
Hours: Mon. through Thur. 9-9, Fri. 9-5:30, Sat. 9-5.
Holdings: Highschool yearbook collection. Local census records from 1790 to 1920. Manuscript collection on the Isles of Shoals. Files of KINSHIP KRONICLE and GOODWIN NEWS. Complete run on microprint of many local newspapers. Municipal records. Cemetery records. Many local church records. Complete file of telephone and city directory. Large book collection. Vertical file. Map collection. Proper name index to the holdings.

St. John's Church, 101 Chapel St., Portsmouth 03801, Telephone 436-8283.
Hours: Mon. through Fri. 9-4.
Holdings: Church records. Genealogical files on members.

Strawberry Banke, Inc., P. O. Box 300, 454 Court St., Portsmouth 03802-0300, Telephone 433-1100.
Hours: By appt.
Holdings: Files on local families that own homes in Strawberry Banke area of the city. Small collection of genealogies. Rockingham County records and census records up to 1820.

Whalley Library, Masonic Temple, 351 Middle St., Portsmouth 03801, Telephone 436-3712.

Hours: Wed. 8-12 & by appt.
Holdings: Files on local past Masons especially from the Langdon family.
Notes and papers of late local historian Gerald Frost.

RAYMOND (1764)
Town Office Bldg., Epping St., Raymond 03077, Telephone 895-4735.
Previous names: Freetown.

Dudley-Tucker Library, P. O. Box 382, Raymond 03077-0382, Telephone 895-2633.
Hours: Winter: Mon. & Thur. 1-8:30, Tues. & Wed. 10-5, Fri. 12-5, Sat. 10-1. Summer: Mon. 1-8:30, Tues. & Wed. 10-5, Thur. 1-6, Fri. 12-5.
Holdings: Small book collection. File of local newspaper RAYMOND TIMES.

Raymond Historical Society, P. O. Box 1764, Raymond 03077, no telephone.
Hours: By appt.
Holdings: Town records. Business records. School records. Cemetery lists.
Files on local families.

RYE (1726)
10 Central Rd., Rye 03870, Telephone 964-8562.
Previous names: Gosport, Panneway, Sandy Beach, Star Island.

Rye Historical Society-see Rye Public Library.

Rye Public Library, P. O. Box 57, 581 Washington Rd., Rye 03870, Telephone 964-8401.
Hours: Mon., Wed., Fri. 9-5, Tues. & Thur. 1-8, Sat. 9-12.
Holdings: Files on local families especially the Philbrook and Locke families. Vertical files. Large book collection. Includes holdings of Rye Historical Society.

SALEM (1750)
Municipal Bldg., 33 Geremonty Dr., Salem 03079, Telephone 893-5731 ext. 142.

Kelly Library, 234 Main St., Salem 03079, Telephone 898-7064.
Hours: Mon. through Fri. 9-9, Sat. 9-5.
Holdings: Some town records. File of local newspaper SALEM OBSERVER.

Salem Historical Society, 43 Lake Shore Rd., Salem 03079-Telephone 898-5660.
Hours: By appt.
Holdings: Town records. Pre-1936 deeds. Civil War pension application forms. Papers of several late local historians.

SANDOWN (1756)
Town Hall, 320 Main St., Sandown 03873, Telephone 887-4870.

Sandown Historical Society and Museum, P. O. Box 77, Sandown 03873, no telephone.
Hours: By appt.
Holdings: Small collection of Civil War diaries. Cemetery lists.

SEABROOK (1768)
P. O. Box 4, Seabrook 03874, Telephone 474-3152.

Brown Library, 636 Lafayette Rd., Seabrook 03874-9501, Telephone 474-2044.
Hours: Mon., Wed., Fri. 12-8, Tues. & Thur. 10-6, Sat. 9-1 (no Sat. hours in summer).
Holdings: Small book collection. Files on local families. Town records on microfilm. Records of many local groups. Files of four defunct newspapers. Chase family papers. Includes holdings of the Historical Society of Seabrook.

Historical Society of Seabrook-see Brown Library.

SOUTH HAMPTON (1742)
304 Main Ave., South Hampton 03827, Telephone 394-7696.

South Hampton Public Library, RFD 2, Box 256, South Hampton 03827, Telephone 394-7319.
Hours: Winter: Mon. 7-9, Wed. 12:30-4 & 7-9, Thur. 10:30-3. Summer: Mon. 7-9, Wed. 1-7.
Holdings: Files on local families. Small book collection. Some town records.

STRATHAM (1716)
10 Bunker Hill Ave., Stratham 03885, Telephone 772-4741.
Previous names: Winnicott.

Stratham Historical Society, 218 Portsmouth Ave., Stratham 03885, no telephone.
Hours: By appt.
Holdings: School records. Town records. Files on the Gowen and Pearson families. Records of many local groups especially the Winnicutt Grange. Papers and notes of two late local historians, Margaret Tate and J. Fred Emery.

Wigin Memorial Library 158 Portsmouth Ave., Stratham 03885, Telephone 772-4346.
Hours: Mon. 1-5, Wed. & Fri. 10-12 & 1-8, Sat. 10-1 (Sat. closed in summer)
Holdings: Small book collection.

WINDHAM (1741)
3 North Lowell Rd., Windham 03087, Telephone 434-5075.

Nesmith Library, 3 N. Lowell Rd., Windham 03087, Telephone 432-7154.
Hours: Mon. through Thur. 10-8, Fri. 10-6, Sat. 10-3 (no Sat. hours in summer.
Holdings: Small book collection.

STRAFFORD COUNTY

Registrar of Deeds
P. O. Box 799
Justice & Administration Bldg.
County Farm Rd.
Dover 03820
Telephone 742-1741

Registrar of Probate
P. O. Box 799
Justice & Administration Bldg.
County Farm Rd.
Dover 03820
Telephone 742-2550

BARRINGTON (1722)
Province Lane, Barrington 03825, Telephone 664-5476.

Barrington Historical Society-see Barrington Public Library.

Barrington Public Library, Star RT, Barrington 03825, Telephone 664-9715.
Hours: Mon. 9:30-4:30 & 7-9, Tues., Thur., & Fri. 9:30-4:30, Wed. 7-9, Sun 2-4:30.
Holdings: Holdings of the Barrington Historical Society (small book collection).

*DOVER (1623)

Municipal Bldg., 288 Central Ave., Dover 03820, Telephone 743-6000.
Previous names: Bristol, Cocheco, Hilton's Point, Newichwannock, Northam.

Annie Woodman Institute of Dover, Central Ave., Dover 03820, Telephone
742-1038.
Hours: Tues. through Sat. 2-5.
Holdings: Town records. Records of several local cotton mills. Files of
several defunct local newspapers.

Dover Public Library, 73 Locust St., Dover 03820-3785, Telephone 743-
6050.
Hours: Winter: Mon. through Thur. 9-8:30, Fri. 9-5:30, Sat. 9-5. Summer:
Mon. through Wed. 9-8:30, Thur. & Fri. 9-5, Sat. 9-2.
Holdings: 4000 volumes on town and family history. Microfilm and bound
volumes of numerous defunct local newspapers. Scrapbook collection. Some
town records. Cemetery records. File of GENEALOGICAL RECORD OF
STRAFFORD COUNTY. Includes holdings of the Strafford Genealogical Society

Northam Colonists Historical Society, RT 1, Box 449, Dover 03820, Telephone 742-4674.
Hours: Mon. through Thur. 9-8:30, Fri. 9-5:30, Sat. 9-5.
Holdings: Files on early colonists. Records of volunteer fire companies
from the 1860's and 1870's.

Strafford Genealogical Society-see Dover Public Library.

DURHAM (1732)
Town Office, Durham 03824, Telephone 868-5577.
Previous names Oyster River, Oyster River Plantation.

Durham Historical Society, Box 305, Durham 03824, Telephone 868-5436.
Hours: Sept. through June Tues. & Thur. 2-4, July through Aug. Mon.
through Sun. 1-4.
Holdings: Cemetery lists. Files on local families especially the
Sullivan, Hill, Smith, Frost and Thompson families. File of local defunct
newspaper DURHAM RESIDENT ADVERTISER.

Piscataqua Pioneers-see Special Collection, Ezekiel W. Dimond Library.

Special Collection, Exekiel W. Dimond Library, University of New Hampshire
Durham 03824-3592, Telephone 862-1541.
Hours: Mon. through Fri. 8-4:30.
Holdings: Papers of Adams, Stevens, and Thompson families. Durham town
records. District Court records. Files of HISTORICAL NEW HAMPSHIRE, NEW
HAMPSHIRE PROFILES and other publications. Microfiche collection of
New Hampshire newspapers. Holdings of the Piscataqua Pioneers (all New
Hampshire census records on microfilm, large collection of town reports,
collection of land plats and land records for New Hampshire seacoast area,
records of the Hanson Family Asso., records of the Piscataqua Pioneers,
270 town histories and many local historical publications).

FARMINGTON (1798)
Town Hall, Farmington 03835, Telephone 755-3657.
Previous names: Farmington Dock.

Farmington -New Durham Historical Society-see Goodwin Public Library.

Goodwin Public Library, South Main St., Farmington 03835, Telephone 755-
2944.
Hours: Mon. & Wed. 12-8, Tues. & Thur. 2-5, Fri. 12-5, Sat. 9-2.
Holdings: Small book collection. Some town records. Scrapbook collection
Microfilm file of local newspaper FARMINGTON NEWS. Records of First
Congregational Chunch of Farmington. Includes holdings of Farmington-

New Durham Historical Society.

LEE (1765)
Town Hall, 7 Mast Rd., Lee, Durham 03824, Telephone 659-2964.

Lee Historical Society, Lee Town Hall, Lee, Durham 03824, no telephone.
Hours: By appt.
Holdings: Cemetery records. Files on local families.

Town of Lee Library, Mast Rd., Lee, Durham 03824, Telephone 659-2626.
Hours: Tues. 10-5, Wed. 1-4, Thur. 10-4 & 7-9, Sat. 10-1 (no Sat. hours in
summer).
Holdings: Some town records. Small book collection.

MADBURY (1768)
13 Town Hall Rd., Madbury 03820, Telephone 742-5131.
Previous names: Barbadoes.

Madbury Historical Society, RFD 4, Freshet Rd., Dover 03820, no telephone.
Hours: By appt.
Holdings: Files on local families especially the Demerrett, Young and Miles
families. Some town records.

MIDDLETON (1749)
P. O. Box 156, Middleton 03887, Telephone 473-2134.

MILTON (1802)
P. O. Box 180, Milton 03851, Telephone 652-9414.
Previous names: Milton Mills, North East Parish, Palmer's Mills, Third
Parish, Three Ponds.

New Hampshire Farm Museum, P. O. Box 644, Milton 03851, Telephone 652-7840.
Hours: Mid-June-Columbus Day Tues. through Sat. 10-4, Sun. & Mon. 12-4.
Holdings: Family papers of several area farm families especially the Jones
family.
Publications: newsletter (quarterly available at $15 annual membership).

Township of Milton Historical Society, Inc., P. O. Box 631, Milton 03851,
no telephone.
Hours: By appt.
Holdings: Town records. Cemetery lists.

NEW DURHAM (1749)
P. O. Box 11, New Durham 03855, Telephone 859-2091.
Previous names: Cocheco Township.

New Durham Historical Society-see New Durham Public Library/Resource
Center.

New Durham Public Library/Resource Center, P. O. Box 218, 2 Old Bay Rd.,
New Durham 03855, Telephone 859-2201.
Hours: Mon. 12-8, Wed. 11-5, Fri. 12-5, Sat. 10-4.
Holdings: File of area newspapers. Files on local families especially the
Tash, Chesley, Jay and Ricker families. Town records. Records for 124
area graveyards. Vital statistics lists. Record of local Free-Will
Baptist church. Includes holdings of the New Durham Historical Society.

*ROCHESTER (1722)
31 Wakefield St., Rochester 03867, Telephone 332-2130.

Rochester Historical Society, P. O. Box 65, Rochester 03867, no telephone.
Hours: By appt.
Holdings: Cemetery lists. Files on local families.

Rochester Public Library, 65 S. Main St., Rochester 03867, Telephone 332-1428.
Hours: Mon. through Thur. 9:30-9, Fri. 9:30-5, Sat. 9:30-4 (no Sat. hours in summer), Sun. 1-4 (no Sun. hours in summer).
Holdings: Small book collection. Some municipal records. File of City directory. File of local newspaper ROCHESTER COURIER.

ROLLINSFORD (1849)
P. O. Box 384, Rollinsford 03869, Telephone 742-2510.
Previous names: Salmon Falls.

*SOMERSWORTH (1754)
157 Main St., Somersworth 03878, Telephone 692-4262.
Previous names: Sligo, Summersworth.

Somersworth Public Library, 25 Main St., Sumersworth 03878, Telephone 692-4587.
Hours: Mon. through Wed. 10-8:30, Thur. & Fri. 10-5:30, Sat. 10-3.
Holdings: Municipal records. Small book collection. File of city directories. Includes holdings of Summersworth Historical Society of Somersworth.

Summersworth Historical Society of Somersworth-see Somersworth Public Library.

STRAFFORD (1820)
Town Hall, Strafford 03884, Telephone 664-2192.

Hill Library, P. O. Box 130, Center Strafford 03815, Telephone 664-2800.
Hours: Winter: Tues. 12-8, Thur. 9-2, Sat. 10-4. Summer: Tues. 12-9, Thur. 9-2 & 7-9, Sat. 10-4.
Holdings: Cemetery records. Files on local families. Tuttle family diaries. Records of Strafford Union, Cate and Austin-Cate Academy. Scrapbook collection.

SULLIVAN COUNTY

Registrar of Deeds
14 Main St.
Newport 03773
Telephone 863-2110

Registrar of Probate
P. O. Box 417
Newport 03773-0417
Telephone 863-3150

ACWORTH (1752)
Box 15, South Acworth 03607   Telephone 835-6879.
Previous names: Burnet.

Acworth Historical Committee-see Acworth Silsby Public Library.

Acworth Silsby Public Library, P. O. Box 179, Acworth 03601, Telephone 835-2150.
Hours: Tues., Thur., & Sun. 1-4, Thur. 10:30-11:30.
Holdings: Town records. File on local families especially the Metcalfe and Bascom families. Small book collection. Cemetery lists. Includes holdings of the Acworth Historical Committee.

CHARLESTOWN (1753)
P. O. Box 834, Charlestown 03603, Telephone 826-5821.
Previous names: No. #4.

Charlestown Historical Society, Old Town Hall, Charlestown 03603, no telephone.
Hours: By appt.
Holdings: Some town school and church records. Several files of defunct local newspapers.

Old Fort #4 Associates, P. O. Box 336, Charlestown 03603, Telephone 826-5700.
Hours: Late June-Labor Day,.Sun. through Sat. 10-5.
Holdings: Collection of local journals and manuscript files on areas pre-Revolutionary history.

Silsby Free Public Library, Box 307, Main St., Charlestown 03603-0307, Telephone 826-7793.
Hours: Winter: Mon., Wed., Thur. 1-5 &6-8, Tues. & Fri. 10-5. Summer: Mon. 1-5 & 6-8, Tues. through Fri. 10-4.
Holdings: Small book collection.

*CLAREMONT (1764)
City Hall, Claremont 03743, Telephone 542-7000.

Claremont N.H. Historical Society, 26 Mulberry St., Claremont 03743, no telephone.
Hours: Mid-June to Sept. Sun. 1-4.
Holdings: Cemetery lists. Small book collection. Files of local families

Fiske Free Library, 108 Broad St., Claremont 03743, Telephone 542-8943.
Hours: Mon. through Thur. 9-7, Fri. 11-5, Sat. 9-4.
Holdings: Small collection of unpublished family history. Large book collection. Many local newspapers on microfilm dating from 1832. Vertical file.

CORNISH (1765)
P. O. Box 183, Cornish Flat 03476, Telephone 542-2845.
Previous names: Mast Camp.

Cornish Historical Society, RR 3, Box 100, Cornish 03745-9707, no telephone.
Hours: By appt.
Holdings: Cemetery records with index. Files on local families.

George H. Stowell Free Library, P. O. Box 264, Cornish Flat 03746, Telephone 543-3644.
Hours: Mon. & Wed. 3-5 & 6:30 ⇀ 8:30, Fri. 6:30-8:30, Sat. 10-12.
Holdings: Small book collection. Microfilm collection of tax and town records.

CROYDON (1763)
HCR 63, Box 9, Newport 03773, Telephone 863-7830.

GOSHEN (1791)
P. O. Box 710, Goshen 03752, Telephone 863-5655.

Goshen Historical Society- see Olive G. Pettis Library.

Olive G. Pettis Library, P. O. Box 742, Goshen 03752, Telephone 863-6921.
Hours: Mon. 3-6, Wed. 7-9, Sat. 9-12.
Holdings: Town records. Cemetery lists. Papers of the Gunnison and Nelson families. Includes the holdings of the Goshen Historical Society.

GRANTHAM (1761)
P. O. Box 135, Grantham 03753, Telephone 863-5608.
Previous names: New Grantham.

Grantham Historical Society, P. O. Box 540, Grantham 03753, no telephone.
Hours: By appt.
Holdings: Some family papers especially of the Rainey, Barton and Howard
families. Cemetery lists. Records of local granges. Records of local
lending libraries.

LANGDON (1787)
P. O. Box 158A, Alstead 03602, Telephone 835-2389.

LEMPSTER (1735)
P. O. Box 33, Lempster 03605, Telephone 863-3213.
Previous names: Dupplin, No. #9.

Lempster Historical Society, Town Hall, Lempster 03606, no telephone.
Hours: By appt.
Holdings: Some town records.

Miner Memorial Library, Box 131, E. Lempster 03605, no telephone.
Hours: Mon. & Wed. 3-8 (winter only).
Holdings: Some town records.

NEWPORT (1761)
15 Sunapee St., Newport 03773, Telephone 863-2224.
Previous names: Grenville.

Newport Historical Society, 168 Cheney St., Newport 03773. no telephone.
Hours: By appt.
Holdings: Murphy family papers. Files on local families. Several files of
defunct local newspapers.

Richards Free Library, 58 North Main St., Newport 03773, Telephone 863-
3430.
Hours: Mon., Tues., Thur. 10-7, Wed. 10-6, Fri. 10-5, Sat. 10-1.
Holdings: Microfilm collection of early town records. Clipping file.
Small book collection.

PLAINFIELD (1761)
Box 206, Meriden 03770, Telephone 469-3201.

Meriden Town Library, P. O. Box 354, Main St., Meriden 03770-0354, Tele-
phone 469-3252.
Hours: Mon. 2-8, Tues. 3-6, Thur. 10-12 & 2-6, Sat. 10-1.
Holdings: Microfilm collection of town records and local deeds.

Phillip Read Memorial Library, RT 12A, Plainfield 03781, Telephone 675-
6866.
Hours: Mon. 7-9, Wed. 1-5 & 7-9, Fri. 1-5, Sat. 9-12.
Holdings: Files on local families. Some town records and local deeds.
Clipping file.

Plainfield Historical Society, Plainfield 03781, no telephone.
Hours: By appt.
Holdings: Book collection. Cemetery lists. Some town records.

SPRINGFIELD (1769)
Box 87, Springfield 03284, Telephone 763-4805.
Previous names: Prôtectworth.

Springfield Historical Society, P. O. Box 355, West Springfield 03284, no
telephone.
Hours: By appt.
Holdings: Records of Howard Memorial Church. School records. Clipping
file. Vertical file. Hill family papers.

SUNAPEE (1768)

P. O. Box 303, Sunapee 03782, Telephone 763-2449.
Previous names: Corey's Town, Covery's Town, Saville, Wendell.

Abbott Library, P. O. Box 314, Sunapee 03782, Telephone 763-5513.
Hours: Mon. through Wed. 10-8, Thur. & Fri. 10-6, Sat. 10-1.
Holdings: Some town records. Small book collection.

Sunapee Historical Society, P. O. Box 501, Sunapee 03782, no telephone.
Hours: By appt.
Holdings: Cemetery records. File of local defunct newspaper LAKE SUNAPEE
ECHO. Some family papers especially of the George family.

UNITY (1753)

HCR 66, Box 176, Newport 03773, Telephone 542-9665.
Previous names: Buckingham.

Unity Historical Society, HCR 66, Box 176, Newport 03773, no telephone.
Hours: By appt.
Holdings: Town records. Cemetery records. Files on local families.

Unity Free Public Library, HCR 66, Newport 03773, no telephone.
Hours: By appt.
Holdings: Small book collection. Some town records.

WASHINGTON (1735)

P. O. Box 109, Hillsborough 03280, Telephone 495-3667.
Previous names: Camden, Line of Towns #8, Monadnock #8, New Concord.

Shedd Free Library, P. O. Box 95, Hillsborough 03280, Telephone 495-3592.
Hours: Tues. 10-3, Thur. 1-3 & 5-8, Sat. 10-12 (summer only).
Holdings: Small book collection.

Washington Archives Committee-see Washington Historical Society.

Washington Historical Society, Hillsborough 03280, no telephone.
Hours: By appt.
Holdings: Safford family papers. Record of Tubbs Union Academy. Index
card file of vital statistics. Includes holdings of the Washington
Archives Committee.

APPENDIX A: Other institutions with holdings of interest to genealogists.

The following institutions did not get their data to me until the manuscript had been completed.

CCC Museum, Bear Brook State Park, RFD 2, Box 507, Allenstown 03275, no telephone.
Hours: By appt.
Holdings: Records of Civilian Conservation Corp units in New Hampshire.

Hancock Historical Society, Hancock 03449, Telephone 525-9379.
Hours: Wed. 2-4 and Sat. 2-4 (only in summer) and by appt.
Holdings: Clipping file. File of defunct local newspapers. Files on families. Business records.

Hancock Town Library, P. O. Box 130, Main St., Hancock 03449, Telephone 525-4411.
Hours: Tues. & Thur. 10-12 & 1-7, Sat. 10-4.
Holdings: Small book collection.

Lockhaven Schoolhouse, East Hill Rd., Enfield 03748, Telephone 632-4993.
Hours: By appt.
Holdings: School records. Some town records.

Milford Historical Society, 45 Amherst St., Milford 03055, no telephone.
Hours: By appt.
Holdings: Papers of Moore and Hutchinson families.

APPENDIX B: Location of LDS Family History Centers in New Hampshire.

Concord
      90 Clinton Street, 03301
      telephone 225-2848

Nashua
      110 Concord Street, 03060
      telephone 880-7371

Portsmouth
      Andrew Jarvis Drive, 03801
      telephone 433-4428.

APPENDIX C: Bibliography.

General History:

Pillsbury, Hobart, NEW HAMPSHIRE A HISTORY (NYC: Lewis, 1927).

Squires, James D. THE GRANITE STATE OF THE UNITED STATES (NYC: American Historical, 1956).

Turner, Lynn W. THE NINTH STATE (Chapel Hill NC: University of North Carolina, 1983).

Van Deventer, David E. THE EMERGENCE OF PROVINCIAL NEW HAMPSHIRE 1623-1741 (Baltimore: John Hopkins University, 1976).

Genealogical and Biographical Works:

Bell, Charles H. THE BENCH AND BAR OF NEW HAMPSHIRE (Boston: Houghton Mifflin, 1894).

Carter, N. F. NATIVE MINISTRY OF NEW HAMPSHIRE (Concord NH: Rumford, 1906.

Editorial Staff, NEW HAMPSHIRE EDITION, AMERICAN SERIES OF POPULAR BIOGRAPHIES (Boston: New England 1902).
May be inaccurate information.

Editorial Staff, THE NEW HAMPSHIRE GENEALOGICAL RECORD (Bowie MD: Heritage, 1988).

Noyes, Sybil, GENEALOGICAL DICTIONARY OF MAINE AND NEW HAMPSHIRE (Portland ME: Southworth-Anthoesen, 1928-1939).
Data includes references to specific public documents.

Osterlin, Pauline J. NEW HAMPSHIRE MARRIAGE LICENSES AND INTENTIONS (Bowie MD: Heritage 1991).

Potter, Chandler C. THE MILITARY HISTORY OF THE STATE OF NEW HAMPSHIRE 1623-1861 (Baltimore: Genealogical, 1972).

Stearns, Ezra, GENEALOGICAL AND FAMILY HISTORY OF THE STATE OF NEW HAMPSHIRE, A RECORD OF THE ACHIEVEMENTS OF HER PEOPLE IN THE MAKING OF A COMMONWEALTH AND THE FOUNDING OF A NATION (NYC: Lewis 1908). The data in this work should be considered suspect.

Census Data

Holbrook, Jay M. NEW HAMPSHIRE RESIDENTS 1633-1699 (Oxford MA: Holbrook Research Institute, 1979.

_____. NEW HAMPSHIRE 1776 CENSUS (Oxford MA: Holbrook Research Institute, 1976).

_____. NEW HAMPSHIRE 1732 CENSUS (Oxford MA: Holbrook Research Institute, 1981).

Threlfall, John B. HEADS OF FAMILIES AT THE SECOND CENSUS OF THE UNITED STATES TAKEN IN THE YEAR 1800 (Madison WI: privately printed, 1973).

United States Government Printing Office. HEADS OF FAMILIES AT THE FIRST CENSUS OF THE UNITED STATES TAKEN IN THE YEAR 1790 (Washington DC: United States Government Printing Office, 1907).

Jackson, Ronald V. et al. 1890 NEW HAMPSHIRE CENSUS INDEX (N. Salt Lake City UT: Accelerated Indexing, 1985).

_____. NEW HAMPSHIRE 1850 INDEX CENSUS (N. Saltlake City: Accelerated Indexing, 1978).

_____. NEW HAMPSHIRE 1840 INDEX CENSUS (N. Salt Lake City UT: Accelerated Indexing, 1978).

_____. NEW HAMPSHIRE 1860 INDEX CENSUS (N. Salt Lake City UT: Accelerated Indexing, 1986).

_____. 1810 CENSUS INDEX (N. Salt Lake City UT: Accelerated Indexing, 1976).

_____. NEW HAMPSHIRE 1830 INDEX CENSUS (N. Salt Lake City UT: Accelerated Indexing, 1977).

_____. NEW HAMPSHIRE 1820 INDEX CENSUS (N. Salt Lake City: Accelerated Indexing, 1976).

County History:

Child, Hamilton, GAZETTER OF GRAFTON COUNTY (Syracuse NY: Syracuse Journal, 1886).

_____. HISTORY OF CHESHIRE AND SULLIVAN COUNTIES (Syracuse NY: Syracuse Journal, 1886).

Hazlett, Charles A. HISTORY OF ROCKINGHAM COUNTY (Chicago   : Richmond-Arnold, 1915).

Hurd, D. Hamilton HISTORY OF HILLSBOROUGH COUNTY (Philadelphia   : J. W. Lewis, 1885).

_____. HISTORY OF MERRIMACK AND BELKNAP COUNTIES (Philadelphia   : J. W. Lewis, 1885).

Merrill, George D. HISTORY OF CARROLL COUNTY (Boston   : W. A. Fergusson, 1889).

_____. HISTORY OF COOS COUNTY (Boston   : W. A. Fergusson, 1886).

Scales, John. HISTORY OF STRAFFORD COUNTY (Chicago   : Richmond-Arnold, 1914).

Other Reference Works.

Burdick, Linda B. NEW HAMPSHIRE COLLECTIONS: A GUIDE TO OUR CULTURAL HERITAGE. (Concord NH: New Hampshire Historical Society and New Hampshire State Library, 1992).
This is a descriptive guide to special collections held by New Hampshire museums and libraries. Many of the collections described are genealogical holdings or would be of interest to genealogists. It is planned to have subsequent editions which would expand the number of collections and institutions being covered.

Copeley, William INDEX TO GENEALOGIES IN NEW HAMPSHIRE TOWN HISTORIES (Concord NH: New Hampshire Historical Society, 1988).

Editorial Staff, NEW HAMPSHIRE REGISTER 1993 (Concord NH: Tower, 1993).
An annual reference work on the state. It includes villages and com- munities located within incorporated towns and cities.

Haskell Jr., John D. et al. NEW HAMPSHIRE A BIBLIOGRAPHY OF ITS HISTORY (Boston   : G. K. Hall, 1979).
The work includes references to articles that appeared in local

newspapers.

Hunt, Elmer M. NEW HAMPSHIRE TOWN NAMES (Peterborough NH: Noone House, 1970).
The work also refers to names of families involved in founding NH towns as well as discussing previous names of communities.

Jaccand, Robert D. PASSAGES TO FAMILY HISTORY: A GUIDE TO GENEALOGICAL RESEARCH IN THE DARTMOUTH COLLEGE LIBRARY (Hanover NH: Dartmouth College Library, 1990).

New Hampshire State Library. DIRECTORY OF NEW HAMPSHIRE 1993 (Concord: New Hampshire State Library, 1993).
It lists the mailing addresses and telephone numbers of all public and many private libraries. It also includes the home telephone number of the head librarians of public libraries and the chairpersons of the libraries' board of trustees.

The Association of Historical Societies of New Hampshire, Inc. THE ASSOCIATION OF HISTORICAL SOCIETIES OF NEW HAMPSHIRE, INC. 1991-1992 (Concord: The Association of Historical Societies of New Hampshire, Inc., 1992).
This is an annual directory of associations belonging to this organization. It includes mailing addresses of the current officers.

New Hampshire Genealogical Periodicals:

AMERICAN-CANADIAN GENEALOGIST, American-Canadian Genealogical Society, P. O. Box 668, Manchester NH 03105-0668. Quarterly available at $3 per issue.

FAMILY TRACES, Merrimack Valley Society of Genealogists, P. O. Box 1035, Concord NH 03302. Quarterly available with $6 annual membership.

GENEALOGICAL RECORD OF STRAFFORD COUNTY, Strafford Genealogical Society, P. O. Box 322, Dover NH 03820. Bi-monthly available with $10 annual membership.

KINSHIP KRONICLES, Rockingham Society of Genealogists, P. O. Box 81, Exeter NH 03833. Quarterly available with $6.50 annual membership.

NEW HAMPSHIRE GENEALOGICAL RECORD, New Hampshire Society of Genealogists, P. O. Box 2316, Concord NH 03302. Quarterly available with $20 annual dues.

NEWSLETTER, New Hampshire Society of Genealogists, Concord NH 03302. Quarterly available with $20 annual dues.